JUDGE FOR YOURSELF

Steve and Alice Lawhead

This book is designed to help you exercise your ethics and apply them in tough situations. You can read it by yourself or study it with the help of a group. Student activity booklets (Rip-Off Sheets) and a leader's guide with visual aids (SonPower Multiuse Transparency Masters) are available from your local Christian bookstore or from the publisher.

BOOKS a division of SP Publications, Inc.
WHEATON, ILLINOIS 60187

Offices also in
Whitby, Ontario, Canada
Amersham-on-the-Hill, Bucks, England

All Bible quotations are from the *Holy Bible: New International Version*, © 1978 by the New York International Bible Society. Used by permission of Zondervan Bible Publishers.

Library of Congress Catalog Card Number: 84-52039
ISBN: 0-89693-363-6

Recommended Dewey Decimal Classification: 248.83
Suggested Subject Heading: YOUTH—RELIGIOUS LIFE

© 1985, SP Publications, Inc. All rights reserved.
Printed in the United States of America

CONTENTS

1. *Meet the Judge*
7

2. *The Case of the Mangled Monkey*
19

3. *The Case of the Devastated Detective*
31

4. *The Case of the Family Feud*
45

5. *The Case of the Immodest Model*
59

6. *The Case of the Dissenting Deacon*
71

7. *The Case of the Filched Final*
83

8. *The Case of the Gambling Guardian*
95

9. *The Case of the Trusting Trimbles*
105

10. *The Case of the Persecuted Pressman*
119

11. *The Case of the Dubious Detergent*
133

12. *The Case of the Liberated Leader*
145

13. *In Conclusion,
Ladies and Gentlemen of the Jury*
156

Dedicated to the memory of
Arthur L. Slaikeu
1915-1967

1. MEET THE JUDGE

Time: 10 A.M.
Place: Court of Ethical Appeals
Enter: Prosecuting attorney, Ms. Wilhelmena Everworth. It is her duty to prove, beyond a reasonable doubt, that the accused is guilty of breaking one or more moral laws and violating Christian principles.

Appearing from the other side of the courtroom is Mr. McArthur Fitzwilliam, counsel for the defense. Next to him walks the accused, a sincere but confused individual who, with lowered head, mutters, "It seemed like the thing to do at the time." It is Fitzwilliam's responsibility to prove his client's innocence and win a verdict of "not guilty."

Both attorneys will quote Scripture, cite history, and employ cool logic in presenting their arguments.

The bailiff rises and bellows, "Hear, ye! Hear, ye! The Court of Ethical Appeals is now in session. The Honorable Judge Eubie presiding. All rise!"

The judge enters the courtroom and settles down in the worn leather chair behind the massive walnut bench of justice. Applying three masterful strokes with the wooden gavel, the judge says, "This court will come to order." The voice is a familiar one, or should be, because in this court *you* are the judge.

TEST CASE #1

Now you know what this book is about. It puts you in the courtroom, in the most honored position of all. You will be the judge. So get out your gold fountain pen, lean back in your red leather chair and prepare to decide for or against the defendant.

Before you get too comfortable in that red leather chair, remember that the full responsibility for making a fair judgment rests on your shoulders. That's a pretty heavy weight. So take care to listen closely to all the arguments, and keep an open mind to both sides. When all the evidence is in, you can weigh it carefully and decide. After receiving more background information, you may reopen the case and issue a final verdict.

Let's try a test case right now and see how it works.

Through eyewitness testimony, you reconstruct the facts of the case: Mr. Robert Goodyard lived next door to a certain Mr. William Worster. Goodyard kept his yard in tip-top condition. He trimmed his shrubs, manicured the lawn, applied sophisticated weed-killers and fertilizers, and cultivated his elaborate flower gardens.

Worster, on the other hand, spent almost no time on his yard. He let it run wild most of the year and bothered to mow it only once or twice a season. On his lawn, dandelions outnumbered blades of grass three to one, and it was this particular weed that started the trouble. When Worster's dandelions started to take over Goodyard's lawn, Goodyard began to plan his revenge.

Late one August night, Goodyard set fire to Worster's house and garage. Fire fighters arrived just in time to rescue the Worster children from the blazing

MEET THE JUDGE

building, but they were too late to save the property.

Goodyard readily admitted that he started the fire, but claimed it was his perfect right to do so since Worster was such a thoughtless and generally obnoxious next-door neighbor.

The charges: Robert Goodyard is being charged with a lack of compassion. Remember that in your Court of Ethical Appeals, only moral and spiritual judgments are made. The fact that Goodyard is also guilty of arson is not this court's concern. In the Court of Ethical Appeals you are only involved with matters of the heart, sins of the spirit. So, based on the charge against him—that of lacking compassion—what is your verdict?

Guilty?

Not guilty?

OK, that was an easy one. You probably didn't have to spend a lot of time deliberating in chambers before you realized that Goodyard stands guilty as accused. The fact that Worster was an undesirable neighbor is pretty much beside the point. You don't torch a guy's house just because his weeds are getting into your yard, right? Right.

But before you think your judge's job is going to be a cinch, let's alter the situation a little.

TEST CASE #2

It's Goodyard and Worster again.

He wasn't happy, but Goodyard decided to live with the spread of Worster's dandelions into his yard. He was more worried about all the junked cars in his neighbor's driveway and the broken-down condition of the house. He suspected that Worster's house had termites—a threat to every home on the block—and heard from the neighbor kids that there were mice in the house, maybe even rats. When Goodyard finally talked to Worster about the problem, Worster angrily told him to mind his own business and refused to discuss it further.

As the problem got worse, neighborhood parents told their children to stay away from the Worster house for reasons of safety. Finally, when little Johnny Goodyard was frightened by a rat in the alley behind Worster's, Goodyard got fed up. He called city authorities, saying Worster's property violated city codes. A city building inspector examined the house and quickly condemned it. Worster was forced to leave his home because he couldn't afford to repair it. He had to move his family into government-subsidized housing on the other side of town.

Goodyard is now being charged with lacking compassion. What is the verdict, Your Honor?

Guilty?

Not guilty?

This time it isn't so easy to decide. Maybe if Goodyard had taken other steps, Worster wouldn't have lost his home. For example, Goodyard might have spent a few Saturdays helping his neighbor fix up his house. On the other hand, how much should a person have to put up with? Goodyard has his own family to think of. If the Worster house was providing a home for pests and rodents, then there are obviously laws to take care of situations like that.

TEST CASE #3

Now let's complicate things further. Let's say that Goodyard is a Christian man. He doesn't like having a slob for a neighbor, but his biggest concern is that Worster isn't a Christian, and the Worster children are receiving no Christian training. So the Goodyards take the Worster kids to church with them every Sunday, and in the summer they bring them to Vacation Bible

MEET THE JUDGE

School. Mrs. Goodyard invites Mrs. Worster to a women's Bible study that meets weekday mornings, and sometimes Mrs. Worster comes, though not regularly. Over the years, Goodyard has tried to talk to Worster about spiritual matters. But he's been unsuccessful so far in reaching him for Christ, even though he occasionally senses an interest on Worster's part.

Under these circumstances, what is Goodyard's responsibility to report building code violations at Worster's house? Can you see that bringing the authorities down on Worster might cause big problems in the relationship that is growing between the two families? How could the Worster family believe the Goodyards' claims about God, Christ, and love if the Goodyards call in the law?

You see, the real problem here is Christian responsibility. When Christians are in a situation that demands a decision about what to do, they often have a lot more to think about than non-Christians do. And, strangely enough, the same Christian truths we seek to uphold will often be the biggest stumbling blocks to doing the right thing.

So how do we decide how to act in these sticky situations? What guidelines has God given us? All of the moral rules we have (most of them are summed up in the Ten Commandments) are fine as far as they go. The trouble is, they don't always go far enough. Sometimes we get stuck with problems that have so many angles, that we don't know which action is the right one.

ON THE BORDER LINE

Sometimes you find yourself in a tough spot where none of your options look good. Have you ever faced any of the following situations?

- No-win situations—Whatever you do, whatever happens, everyone will come out a loser.
- Six-of-one-and-half-a-dozen-of-the-other situations—Here, both choices are pretty much the same.
- Lesser-of-two-evils situations—There doesn't seem to be a *good* solution to the problem, just two bad things that could happen, one a little less horrible than the other.

Those are pretty gloomy ways to look at moral conflict. Let's try another approach.

Let's call these hard places *borderline cases.* Try to think of a border line in this way: You've decided to go backpacking in the Great Smokey Mountains of North Carolina and Tennessee. On your road map it's obvious where North Carolina leaves off and Tennessee begins because there's an orange line between the two of them. But when you're actually tromping around in the hills, hiking through trees, wading across rivers, and climbing over rocks in the Smokies, there is no orange line on the ground. One state looks pretty much like the other.

Even though you can't tell what state you're in, that doesn't mean there isn't a very definite line that divides North Carolina and Tennessee, or that North Carolina is not a very different place from Tennessee, or that you are not indeed in one state or another. It does mean that though there is a state border, that border is not always as clear as you might like it to be when you're actually there, hiking in the mountains.

When you are in a borderline ethical situation—as Mr. Goodyard was—there is often a similar confusion, but it involves what is the right or the wrong thing to do. You may see the boundary in one place while your friends, parents, or society think that it's somewhere else. The important thing to remember is that there *is* a

MEET THE JUDGE

dividing line, and it is up to you to decide as best you can what is the right thing to do, and then to act on that decision.

Though, to the hiker, the boundary between Tennessee and North Carolina is hard to place, still it is the Great Smokey Mountains themselves that form the line dividing the two states. It is the same with moral and spiritual decisions. The borderline case provides the clearest picture of right and wrong, no matter how blurred and confusing it might seem when we are in the thick of it.

As we live our lives day to day, we know for certain whether some things are right or wrong. You don't strangle your lockermate just because he left his dirty gym clothes in the locker over the weekend, right? And just because you keep from killing him, you shouldn't be too proud of yourself. Such a decision is pretty easy to make—it's expected. Does a soldier get a medal for doing his duty? No, medals are given for the *exceptional*—for courage above and *beyond* the call of duty. Medals are given for making the hard choices and winning battles.

In the Christian life the real battles are fought in the gray areas. Genuine personal growth takes place when we are in very confusing situations—borderline situations—and we use every resource we have to make the right decisions. When we rise to the challenge of working through borderline cases, we show what we're made of. It is on the border line that our faith is tested.

As we navigate the gray areas, we learn in more concrete ways that God cares about us and about what we do. Though it might be a lonely place, we are never alone on the border line. On the contrary, it is there that we are most aware of God's presence in our lives and of our need for His guidance.

Of course, bad things can happen on the border line. We might misread the situations. We might exercise poor judgment. We might make the wrong decisions and make big mistakes. Yet we must face those kinds of risks if we are to grow.

THOU SHALT; THOU SHALT NOT

So, where does that leave all that great moral training we learned? Do all those "shalt's" and "shalt not's" just get thrown out the window?

Absolutely not. We want to state strongly that there is always a *right* thing to do in any given situation based on the commandments that God has given. These commandments are so reliable that even non-Christians accept them as a credible code to live by.

But when the storm of doubt and confusion starts to blow, then we have to throw out all our extra baggage and cling only to what really matters. When Jesus was asked what was the greatest commandment in the Law, He replied:

> *"Love the Lord your God with all your heart and with all your soul and with all your mind." This is the first and greatest commandment. And the second is like it: "Love your neighbor as yourself." All the Law and the Prophets hang on these two commandments* (MATTHEW 22:37-39).

All of the guidelines that your teachers, parents and church have given you ought to be based on these two great commandments. When you were a little kid, you didn't know enough to reason things out for yourself, and it was important for you to remember simple things like "Tell the truth," "Obey your parents," and "Share your toys." These instructions got you through the hard places of childhood.

But as you get older, you have bigger problems and

MEET THE JUDGE 15

more complicated relationships. Not every conflict you meet can be easily resolved by recalling the simple sayings of your childhood.

You're not a kid anymore, and your life is being filled with situations where you must be the judge. The training you have received from your parents, the knowledge you have gained in school, the instruction you have received from your church, your understanding of Scripture, and your belief in God and about people will form the basis of your judgments about life.

YOU BE THE JUDGE

This book will give you a firsthand opportunity to think about the tough moral decisions you make, to consider ethics and spiritual principles, and to find a way that you can decide what is right.

Each chapter in the book presents a case, like the next one, "The Case of the Mangled Monkey." First, the facts of the case are given: who is involved, what happened, and so forth. As you read each case, remember that the main character is a Christian who must keep in mind his or her special spiritual considerations.

Next, the attorneys present their arguments. Imagine that the prosecuting attorney is Wilhelmena Everworth, whom we introduced earlier. It is her job to state which ethical crime has been committed and tell why she believes the defendent is guilty. While legal courts consider crimes such as grand theft and murder, we'll be looking at "moral crimes" such as immodesty or disloyalty or poor stewardship. Remember that a Christian should have higher moral standards than the rest of the world. Even though his or her actions might not be challenged in a regular court of law, they must be addressed by our Court of Ethical Appeals.

After the prosecution rests, Defense Attorney McArthur Fitzwilliam will argue his case. He will do his best to break down the prosecution's arguments, defending his client's actions and explaining why his client is innocent.

Both the prosecution and defense will typically quote or refer to Scripture to support their cases. They will make logical arguments, use careful reasoning, and thoroughly examine the issues involved. On the whole, you can believe what they say to be true, though they may get a little sarcastic or frustrated with each other.

NOW IT'S YOUR TURN

When each argument has been presented, it's up to you, the judge. You alone determine if the accused is guilty or innocent. You must decide, and then issue a statement explaining your verdict. That is, you must say why you decided as you did.

But you're not finished yet. The verdict will be appealed and the case reopened. We'll step back and try to get some more background information on the case. We'll ask key questions, and toy with the idea of "what if?" in trying to see if another outcome to the case would have been more satisfactory.

Finally, we'll look for a personal application to what we've learned. This is where you slip out of your black robe, step down from the judicial bench, and put yourself in the place of the accused. What would *you* have done in a similar situation? How does this situation touch *your* life? We don't want you to merely sit in judgment; we want you to learn from what you've seen.

When the appeal is finished, you should have more insight and understanding, and you'll get one last chance to give your verdict: guilty or not guilty. Maybe you'll change your mind. Maybe you won't. At any rate, you should have a better idea of why you made your decision.

MEET THE JUDGE 17

Ready to take on your first case, Your Honor? As soon as you move on to the next chapter, court is in session.

2. THE CASE OF THE MANGLED MONKEY

THE FACTS OF THE CASE

B.F. Henderson was a wealthy businessman who owned one of the world's finest private collections of Oriental art. His holdings included beautiful jade carvings and silk paintings from the ancient Ch'Ing Dynasty. After watching a television program about a local evangelist's work in Third World countries, Henderson was convinced he should make a large contribution. He decided to donate the most valuable piece in his collection to the evangelist, so the money from its sale could pay for much-needed food and medical supplies. He estimated that the piece would sell for half a million dollars.

Henderson called the Rev. Charles Thompson and told him of his plans. "This is a very generous gift," said the preacher. "Are you sure you wish to do this?"

"Absolutely," replied Henderson. "I feel very strongly that God wants me to be part of your fine work, and this is a way I can do just that."

The next day Pastor Thompson drove to Henderson's mansion on the outskirts of town to take possession of the art object. He was shown a wonderful green carving trimmed in gold and set with dozens of sparkling gems. The gold glimmered against the cool green jade; tiny faceted rubies winked red in the light.

"This is a Sufi temple idol. It's the image of the monkey god, Omin. Very rare. This one is 1,200 years old and considered a wonderful specimen."

Pastor Thompson paused from his examination of the stunningly beautiful statuette. Did you say this is an *idol*?

"Yes, an idol. Also a rare treasure." Henderson was not at all prepared for the preacher's hesitant reaction to his generous gift.

"Mr. Henderson, I have deep reservations about accepting this. God would not approve of furthering His holy work with money from the sale of a pagan idol. This object has been dedicated to a heathen god. How could I dedicate a pagan object to the Lord's work? It just wouldn't be right."

With a good deal of strain between them, the two men parted company. The idol stayed in Henderson's possession.

Three days later Henderson called Pastor Thompson once again. "I've had a change of heart," he said. "I'd like you to come over to the house this afternoon. We have work to do."

When they met again, it was with a unified spirit. They took the jade monkey outside, laid it on the concrete driveway, and proceeded to smash it with hammers until the priceless jade was a fine powder, the gold mangled, and the rubies lost in the rubbish.

CHARGES: The two men are accused of exercising poor stewardship in the use of their God-given resources and mutilating a rare art object.

THE CASE OF THE MANGLED MONKEY

THE ARGUMENTS

PROSECUTION: These men are guilty of destroying a priceless object of art for no good reason. Not only did they ruin a piece of culture and history which can never be replaced, but they denied suffering people the chance to be fed, clothed, and sheltered with money from the sale of the jade monkey.

There was no power in the idol; it represented no true god. It was merely an artifact from a culture long ago, an item of beauty, and part of the great and rich history of humankind. As Christians they had nothing to fear from a bit of stone, some gold, and gems. While Mr. Henderson and Pastor Thompson might be uncomfortable possessing such objects, they overstepped their responsibilities and rights when they decided for generations past and future to destroy something which rightfully belongs to all of us.

If they did not wish to have the statue in their personal possession, they should have sold it for the highest possible price and used the proceeds for the Lord's work. That would have been the Christlike thing to do. The Apostle Paul said that it was acceptable for Christians to eat meat which had been used in pagan ceremonies or which had been offered to idols. Wouldn't it be even more acceptable to feed starving people with the money obtained from the sale of the mangled monkey?

DEFENSE: These men are guilty only of leading their lives in obedience to God. They may not have chosen a popular course, but they chose the right one. For this they should be praised.

God is not impressed by our possessions, but He is pleased by a life that is totally devoted to Him. These men showed courage when they overlooked the dollar value of the pagan object to see that idols are an offense to God. In times past, God's people have been instructed to destroy their pagan gods if they would serve Him. There is no place for any such object in the lives of His people. While possessing the monkey might seem harmless on the surface, there is a subtle and evil power to be reckoned with—Satan. As a tool of the devil, the idol is like the Ouija board, Tarot cards, horoscopes, and all other pagan and occult paraphernalia. It serves no healthy purpose and must be destroyed.

The money that might have come from selling the idol is not needed. God will work out His plan in the world; He will take care of His creation and do it without the help of the devil. The two men were perfectly in tune with God's will when they mangled the monkey.

YOU BE THE JUDGE

What is your verdict? Do you find for the:
- ☐ Prosecution?
- ☐ Defense?

Why? Explain your reasoning.

CASE BACKGROUND

Idolatry, the worship of other gods, was a continuing problem for the early Jews of Israel. It was such a recurring sin that its condemnation was included in the Ten Commandments: *"You shall not make for yourself an idol in the form of anything in heaven above or on the earth beneath or in the waters below"* (EXODUS 20:4).

In its argument, the defense referred to this Scripture from the Law: *"The images of their gods you are to burn in the fire. Do not covet the silver and gold on them, and do not take it for yourselves, or you will be ensnared by it, for it is detestable to the Lord your God"* (DEUTERONOMY 7:25). Following that command means

THE CASE OF THE MANGLED MONKEY

possessions. We have no reason to assume that any were too tainted to be used in the Lord's work.

KEY QUESTIONS

Let's take another look at the "Case of the Mangled Monkey," probe beneath the surface, and examine several key points. How would you answer these questions?

1. Is it important that the idol was worth half a million dollars? What if the object was worth only ten dollars? Would there still be an issue as to whether or not it should be smashed?

2. If Henderson had sold the idol and donated the proceeds to Pastor Thompson without telling him where the money came from, what would have been the outcome? Would any harm have been done to the mission work as a result of using tainted money?

3. Is it important that the monkey was an irreplaceable object of art? Would it be acceptable to smash a worthless idol but not a valuable one? Is an object such as the mangled monkey the same thing as a resource or a talent that God gives to His people for their wise use and caretaking?

4. What would have happened if Mr. Henderson had kept the piece in his possession? As a Christian, would his witness and life have been weakened or compromised through the presence of the object in his home? Does it have an indwelling evil power which could hamper his effectiveness without his knowledge?

5. Can you think of any other action the two men might have taken short of destroying the idol?

THE FINAL ANALYSIS

The strongest biblical case for destroying the Sufi temple god would rest heavily on Old Testament passages, which speak directly to the issue of idolatry and false worship on many occasions. First, the Jews were not to make or worship idols; they were never allowed to build a representation of God to use in their worship of Him. Second, they were to have no close contact with idols. For example, they were forbidden to marry the daughters of Baal, prostitutes whose services were performed in connection with temple worship of Baal. Finally, they were not to possess any pagan idols, whether they belonged to family members, servants, or themselves. Whether or not the Israelites were actually worshiping the pagan god made no difference. They simply were not to have any such objects in their possession.

In the New Testament, however, we find a slight change of attitude. For example, when Paul was in Athens, a city full of idols, he found an altar "To an Unknown God." He used the altar as an opportunity to say that he had news of the "Unknown God," and he shared the Gospel message with those who wanted to hear it (ACTS 17:16-34). Later, in his letter to the Corinthians, he argues against the idea that idols have any power or that a sacrifice to an idol has any meaning, though he goes on to say that close association with such things is something to be discouraged.

But the most important issue in the "Case of the Mangled Monkey" is not idol-worship. Neither Mr. Henderson nor Pastor Thompson were tempted in any way to worship a 1,200-year-old object which had no meaning to them. For this reason it might be argued that Scriptures denouncing idols are less applicable today than when they were written, because times have changed and pagan worship of statues is not a major issue in the life of today's Christian. What we *are* concerned with is living a holy life and determining what interferes with a holy life.

Holy means "set apart for God." Can a person who

THE CASE OF THE MANGLED MONKEY

the precious jade, gold, and rubies of the monkey idol could not be used—even in broken pieces.

In New Testament days the problem of idol-worship had Christians arguing about eating the meat of animals which had been sacrificed to pagan gods and then sold in the general marketplace of Corinth. Many Christians of the day thought the practice of eating this meat was an offense against God, and they condemned the practice for other Christians too. The Apostle Paul addressed the question:

> *Therefore, my dear friends, flee from idolatry. . . . Do I mean then that a sacrifice offered to an idol is anything, or that an idol is anything? No, but the sacrifices of pagans are offered to demons, not to God, and I do not want you to be participants with demons. You cannot drink the cup of the Lord and the cup of demons too; you cannot have a part in both the Lord's table and the table of demons. . . . "Everything is permissable"—but not everything is beneficial. "Everything is permissable"—but not everything is constructive. . . . Eat anything sold in the meat market without raising questions of conscience, for "The earth is the Lord's, and everything in it."*
>
> *If some unbeliever invites you to a meal and you want to go, eat whatever is put before you without raising questions of conscience. But if anyone says to you, "This has been offered in sacrifice," then do not eat it, both for the sake of the man who told you and for conscience' sake—the other man's conscience, I mean, not yours. For why should my freedom be judged by another's conscience? If I take part in the meal with thankfulness, why am I denounced because of something I thank God for?*

> *So whether you eat or drink or whatever you do, do it all for the glory of God. Do not cause anyone to stumble, whether Jews, Greeks or the church of God* (1 CORINTHIANS 10:14, 19-21, 23, 25-32).

Paul's explanation ends with the heart of his counsel: cause no offense to man and glorify God. In the "Case of the Mangled Monkey" each side could use some of Paul's words as a basis for their opinion. The prosecution might say that if the proceeds of the sale of the monkey are *"all to the glory of God,"* then nothing else matters. But the defense would point out that, *"You cannot drink the cup of the Lord and the cup of demons too,"* and that the destruction of the *"demon"* object becomes more important than anything else.

In the Book of Acts, James is quoted as saying, concerning Gentile converts: *"Instead we should write to them, telling them to abstain from food polluted by idols"* (ACTS 15:20).

In 1 John 5:21 we read this: *"Dear children, keep yourselves from idols."*

Turning to the Old Testament, we see King David, the conquerer of many nations, dedicating to God the spoils of his victory over his godless enemies: *"Joram brought with him articles of silver and gold and bronze. King David dedicated these articles to the Lord, as he had done with the silver and gold from all the nations he had subdued"* (2 SAMUEL 8:10-11).

In Matthew 19:21, Jesus' message to the rich young ruler was this: *"If you want to be perfect, go, sell your possessions and give to the poor, and you will have treasure in heaven. Then come, follow Me."* We might assume that some of the young ruler's property would have been obtained in ways unpleasing to Christ. Yet there was no reference made as to the nature of the

THE CASE OF THE MANGLED MONKEY

is determined to be set apart for God have contact with an object which was at one time used in worship completely opposed to God's supreme power and commands?

Let's explore another issue related to this case: the wise and careful management of all of our life's resources—time, energy, and money. The valuable idol was in Mr. Henderson's posssession and could be considered a part of what God had given him to oversee.

We are familiar with the Story of the Talents (MATTHEW 25:14-30), where the worthless servant was condemned and thrown into the darkness because he did not increase his master's holdings by wisely managing the resources entrusted to his care. Might Henderson and Thompson earn similar reproof since they destroyed something which could have been used to bring the Gospel to the unsaved, food to the hungry, clothes to the naked, and shelter to the homeless?

In light of the plight of millions on this earth who do not have what they need to survive, in deference to the many who are hungry and who will die from unfilled needs, might the issue of idols be set aside in favor of the commandment to love one another and help those in need? It would be ironic and perhaps fitting that an art object with pagan roots would fall into the hands of Christians who would use it for the cause of Christ.

BRINGING IT HOME: THE APPLICATION

Does the "Case of the Mangled Monkey" sound a bit exotic? Slightly farfetched? You probably have no gem-encrusted idols in your possession and are not considering a half-million-dollar donation to a world relief organization in any event.

But think about the many youth leaders and traveling evangelists today who encourage young people to burn their rock music albums, destroy their Ouija boards, and quit taking the daily newspaper which prints horoscopes. They argue that there is an evil power contained in these objects which should not be a part of a Christian's life.

Many people who have cleared their lives of such questionable influences report a tremendous load lifted off their shoulders, a freeing experience as though they were bound up to the devil through the possession of these things.

Others, however, experience no such effect and eventually feel only remorse over the destruction of their personal possessions. They feel cheated or misled by those in positions of influence over them, and often become cynical or distrustful because they have been made to act foolishly.

Who is right?

This is a question that confronts all Christians sooner or later, as it touches on the core of what it means to be a mature Christian. It is a question of values and investments.

You can often tell what a person values most in life by seeing where he invests his time, energy, and money. Human beings are made in such a way that faith in God must be an ongoing process if it is to thrive. That means a constant investment and reinvestment of personal resources—in other words, stewardship. Unfortunately, it is a process easily cut off by material things.

"Idols" of various types can take God's place before we're aware of them. It is no longer merely a matter of worshiping a jade monkey; it's more complicated than that. What might be OK for one person causes another to lose sight of God. That's why Paul said, *"Everything is permissable, but not everything is beneficial"* (1 CORINTHIANS 10:23).

It is up to each person to search out his or her own heart, differentiate between what is beneficial and constructive to faith and what is a barrier, and then nurture the helpful attitudes and root out the unhealthy.

Still, Christians do not live in a vacuum. We live in a greater world that has need of the things we can give. Our resources belong not to ourselves alone, but are on loan from God, for use in helping others.

In times past, evangelist Billy Graham has been criticized for using money from non-Christians to aid his ministry. His response has been that money is morally neutral, and that it is in God's power to use any means available to further the cause of Christ. Mr. Graham can run his organization with money from non-Christians as well as Christians. It's all the same to the person who attends one of his crusades and receives Christ because of the message he hears.

Maturity, then, requires a keen sense of balance—juggling the claims of personal values and investment with the needs of a hungry world. In the end we are to honor God in whatever we do.

THE APPEAL: REOPENING THE CASE

Now go back and reread the "Case of the Mangled Monkey" at the beginning of this chapter. Once again, give your verdict and the reasoning behind your decision.

Do you find for the:
☐ Prosecution?
☐ Defense?
Why?

Did your decision change? Did your reasoning?

3. THE CASE OF THE DEVASTATED DETECTIVE

THE FACTS OF THE CASE

Michael Ortiz, detective for the Miami Police Department, sat on a wobbly chair outside Captain Spanel's office. As he stared blankly at the police station's tile walls, he wondered if he was on the edge of giving up everything he had worked so hard for.

Michael's troubles had begun last March when he took on a special assignment to crack a major criminal network that was smuggling Columbian cocaine into the United States. His job: to play the role of Raymond Shada, a high-rolling drug dealer from Milwaukee setting himself up in the drug business in Miami. His real purpose: to work his way through the local drug network and get the hard evidence needed to convict a major drug trafficker known only as "Luiz."

That was five months ago. In that time he had moved out of his apartment and away from his wife, taking up residence in a downtown hotel where he ran his drug business. As Shada, Michael hired prostitutes to entertain out-of-town contacts and had engaged street kids as couriers. He had turned in his Levis and sweatshirts for leather jackets and diamond rings. He had made a name for himself—for Raymond Shada—by flashing $100 bills wherever he went, getting whatever he wanted.

As time went on, it became difficult for Michael to separate his real personality from the character he had created. He almost never phoned his wife, and when he did, he lied to her about his work. His life of Little League, church potluck suppers, and weekends at his parents' house faded while the wild lifestyle of Raymond Shada took over.

The events of last night, though, had shocked him back into himself. Finally, after what seemed like hours of waiting, Michael was called into the captain's office where he let the whole story pour out.

"It happened last night when my partner, George, and I were waiting in a back alley for Luiz to deliver the cocaine. A teenage kid—couldn't have been more than sixteen or seventeen—showed up instead. George stood guard while I inspected the merchandise. When I tasted it, I knew that they had cut the cocaine. It was inferior stuff and not worth the money we were paying for it. At first I didn't know what to do. But then I decided that Raymond Shada would know the quality of the stuff, and Raymond Shada wouldn't let Luiz get away with it. So I told George what was up.

"Right in front of my eyes, George pulled out his .350 Magnum and shot that innocent kid six times in the head, grabbed the coke from me, and ran."

Michael paused; Captain Spanel said nothing. "I stayed behind and looked after the kid. He was dead, of course, and at that point there was nothing I could do."

Michael threw a nylon sports wallet on the desk. "Here's his ID. What a stupid waste of life."

"Mike, I'm sorry it happened. But you know it

THE CASE OF THE DEVASTATED DETECTIVE

wasn't your fault."

"Oh, sure. I mean, I was only doing my job, right? And if an innocent kid gets killed because I didn't try to help, well, that's just too bad."

"Mike, I know this isn't an easy assignment. But you can't blame yourself—"

"I *do* blame myself! I've had it, Captain! I've had it with hanging around bars boozing until they kick me out. I'm sick of pimping for these creeps and making money for the kind of scum that sells dope to grade-school kids. I can't keep lying to everyone and worrying Janelle until she's sick. I hate Raymond Shada, and I won't be him anymore. I've sunk to their level."

"No you haven't. You're doing a *job*. Unfortunately, some people are going to get hurt if we hope to stop these drugs. That's tough. But it's all for a good cause; that's what is important in the long run."

"Captain, I won't do it anymore. I want you to take me off the case."

"Mike, it's too late to take you off. I just can't."

"Then I quit."

CHARGES: Detective Ortiz is accused of failing to carry out his obligation to the public in the war against drug dealing.

THE ARGUMENTS

PROSECUTION: Michael Ortiz is clearly guilty of refusing to do his moral duty. Undercover operations like Michael's are almost the *only* way to get evidence that will convict drug dealers. It may be a "dirty" business, but someone's got to do it.

When "Raymond Shada" was drinking, hiring prostitutes, and making drug buys, *Michael Ortiz* was not truly participating. It was only a role for him, and while in that role he was not responsible for Raymond Shada's actions.

Michael's backing out of the case was short-sighted and selfish. He shouldn't be allowed to destroy months of work and planning and ruin the department's chances of catching "Luiz" just because the going got a little tough. It is his job to do this sort of work; he is a professional. He should not have taken the assignment if he could not handle it. Once he did, though, it was his duty to follow through.

The price of conquering evil must be paid when a greater good is at stake. Does a doctor refuse to perform surgery because some healthy tissue might be removed along with the cancerous tissue? Does a general leading an army refuse to arm himself against the enemy because he is squeamish about viewing the death and destruction caused by his weapons? Of course not.

Michael Ortiz was doing the right thing until he quit the case. It was then that he lost sight of the big picture. As a Christian, he should have been willing to do anything to end the drug traffic that kills thousands of truly innocent people every year.

DEFENSE: Michael Ortiz finally learned an important lesson: that the end does not justify the means. He did the right thing by quitting the case and the force when he realized that he was denying his own moral standards.

It's one thing to be a part of a "sting" operation in an effort to catch and convict criminals. It is another thing entirely to get sucked into the evil of a situation until you are yourself a knowing participant.

Christians are not asked to give up their moral standards and give in to evil for any reason. Can you imagine Christ standing idly by while a seventeen-year-old boy is shot and killed? Do you suppose He would later defend

THE CASE OF THE DEVASTATED DETECTIVE

His actions—or inaction—on the basis of a "greater good"? No! Human life is too valuable to sacrifice—even for the most noble purposes.

Finally, we must keep in mind the Apostle Paul's instruction to hate what is evil and cling to what is good. In battling evil, you cannot "fight fire with fire." This strategy only increases wrongdoing. The way to do away with the darkness of evil is to shine the light of goodness on it. When a Christian commits such sins as drunkenness, adultery, and dishonesty, and excuses these actions in the name of a greater good, then it is time to stop such behavior. Michael Ortiz finally woke up to this fact, and made the right decision in leaving the case.

YOU BE THE JUDGE

What is your verdict? Do you find for the:
☐ Prosecution?
☐ Defense?
Why? Explain your reasoning.

CASE BACKGROUND

In the Bible we see many examples of human life being sacrificed so that evil may be destroyed. The Old Testament describes bloodshed and violence committed by Israelites acting on God's orders.

For instance, the Book of Joshua tells of a man who was ordered by God to destroy the heathen nations living in the Promised Land of Canaan. Joshua and his troops defeated six nations and thirty-one kings, and all of these battles are described as bloody ordeals. The old spiritual, "Joshua Fit the Battle of Jerico" is an upbeat song, but the real story tells of mass destruction. Here's how it really happened:

> *When the trumpets sounded, the people shouted, and at the sound of the trumpet, when the people gave a loud shout, the wall collapsed; so every man charged straight in, and they took the city. They devoted the city to the Lord and destroyed with the sword every living thing in it—men and women, young and old, cattle, sheep and donkeys* (JOSHUA 6:20-21).

And what was God's response to this destruction? We read: *"So the Lord was with Joshua, and his fame spread throughout the land"* (JOSHUA 6:27).

This was in line with what God told the Israelites about how to wage war against the heathen:

> *However, in the cities of the nations the Lord your God is giving you as an inheritance, do not leave alive anything that breathes. Completely destroy them—the Hittites, Amorites, Canaanites, Perizzites, Hivites and Jebusites—as the Lord your God has commanded you. Otherwise, they will teach you to follow all the detestable things they do in worshiping their gods, and you will sin against the Lord your God* (DEUTERONOMY 20:16-18).

We might compare the enemies of God in Joshua's time to the heartless drug traffickers of our day. It could be argued that these dealers' lives must be sacrificed, if necessary, to put an end to the damage they do through drugs and related violence.

The prosecution infers that we must sometimes perform distasteful acts in order to serve God and do what is ultimately good. The Bible has many examples of godly people acting in ways that we would judge immoral. But these acts are done out of obedience to God.

And Christ did say: *"Nothing outside a man can*

THE CASE OF THE DEVASTATED DETECTIVE 37

make him 'unclean' by going into him. Rather, it is what comes out of a man that makes him 'unclean'" (MARK 7:15).

Perhaps this might mean that Michael Ortiz was not immoral or "unclean" in breaking certain moral laws since he was not following his own will but doing his duty to catch the drug smugglers.

On the other hand, the life of Christ serves as the basis of the defense's argument that evil leads to more evil and that the only way to destroy evil is to do what is good. In Christ's time on earth He did not use force even when it was used against Him. His suffering and death reveal a Man who did not defend Himself, but let Himself be beaten, mocked, tortured, and crucified. Christ's goodness in the face of this evil had a strong impact on some onlookers:

> *And when the centurion, who stood there in front of Jesus, heard His cry and saw how He died, he said, "Surely this man was the Son of God!"* (MARK 15:39)

The defense would rather see Michael Ortiz fight the evil of drug smuggling and selling by helping to change the lives and attitudes of the people involved with drugs. That approach would be more Christlike than Michael's taking part in sinful activities to get evidence against the drug dealers.

These words from Paul back up the defense's argument:

> *Love must be sincere. Hate what is evil; cling to what is good. . . . Bless those who persecute you; bless and do not curse. . . . Do not repay anyone evil for evil. Be careful to do what is right in the eyes of everybody. . . . If it is possible, as far as it*

depends on you, live at peace with everyone. Do not take revenge, my friends, but leave room for God's wrath, for it is written: It is mine to avenge; I will repay," says the Lord. On the contrary: "If your enemy is hungry, feed him; if he is thirsty, give him something to drink. In doing this you will heap burning coals on his head." Do not be overcome by evil, but overcome evil with good (ROMANS 12:9, 14, 17-21).

These challenging words describe a Christian who lives totally in God's will. Let's return to the question of one individual Christian, Michael Ortiz, and explore how he should have behaved in this puzzling case.

KEY QUESTIONS

It's hard not to feel sorry for Michael Ortiz—caught between doing his job and giving up his Christian values. But the tough question must still be asked: was he right to quit such an important assignment? To get closer to the answer, you'll need to ask yourself some more questions:

1. Does a Christian have any place on a police force in this country, knowing that he or she will be required to carry and use a deadly weapon?

2. Is there another role in the undercover investigation that Michael Ortiz might have played in order to catch Luiz? Perhaps one that would not require him to lie, cheat, drink, sell drugs? Did he take things too far by hanging around in bars, arranging for prostitutes, and actually making drug buys? Can you accept his behavior without question as a necessary part of his job, or do you think that he could have worked undercover without participating in these activities?

3. What does it mean to be a professional, as when

THE CASE OF THE DEVASTATED DETECTIVE

the prosecution said, "It is his job to do this sort of work; he is a professional"? Does being a professional mean that he will behave differently than someone who is not? Can that ever be an excuse for doing wrong?

4. What is a person's duty to his employer? What was Michael Ortiz's duty to the police force and to the work and planning that had gone into setting up the undercover operation?

5. Are there any situations where it is acceptable to take another person's life? Imagine that Michael Ortiz had been the one with the gun at the drug exchange and that his "partner" George had ordered *him* to kill the courier. What then? Would he have been justified in killing the teenager in order to protect his cover?

6. Do you believe that the courier was "innocent"? Apparently he was paid by Luiz but not personally involved in the drug deal. Do you find yourself saddened, or unaffected, by his death? Would you feel differently about him if he was thirty years old? Twelve years old? A girl? Did the courier deserve what he got?

7. Do you think that fighting the crime of drug trafficking can be compared to fighting a war? If so, does that make a difference to you in what is acceptable and what is unacceptable action?

8. How could Michael Ortiz have fought evil with good and "shined the light of goodness" on Luiz, George, and the others involved in the smuggling? In what practical way do you imagine he might have done that?

9. What were the other alternatives open to Michael Ortiz, short of quitting the force?

THE FINAL ANALYSIS

Perhaps the primary issue in the "Case of the Devastated Detective" is this: does the end justify the means? We don't think a businessman should cheat on his taxes so that he'll have more money to give to missions, or that a churchgoer should break the speed limit in order to make it to the morning worship service on time. So, when the question is asked out of the blue, we reply no.

But when we watch "Magnum P.I." on television, or "Simon and Simon," or "Remington Steele," or any other number of "find-the-bad-guys" shows, we are often unaware of the ethical problems presented when the hero lies about his identity, breaks into a suspect's home or hotel room, steals his car, attacks him physically, and generally uses whatever means he can to capture the criminal. When television is criticized for "immorality," critics are more likely to focus on sex and violence than to question the methods that police or detectives use to catch the crook.

In our case, the prosecution argues that stopping the drug smugglers is all-important because if illegal drugs don't get into this country, they won't go on to ruin the lives of people who use them. Responsible Christians should have an interest in cutting off drug traffic. The prosecution points to examples in Scripture where great evil was fought with determination, loss of human life, and sometimes with an apparent compromise of ethical standards. The prosecution asks, "Is it really compromising if you can keep in mind the evil you are fighting and recognize that you must step outside your true self to put a halt to sinful behavior?"

In contrast, the defense says that a look at the life of Christ and New Testament standards show that immorality and the taking of human life are no longer acceptable—no matter *what* evil is being fought. In the Sermon on the Mount, Christ says:

> *You have heard that it was said, "Eye for eye, and tooth for tooth." But I tell you, Do not resist an evil person. . . . I tell you: Love your enemies and*

THE CASE OF THE DEVASTATED DETECTIVE 41

pray for those who persecute you, that you may be sons of your Father in heaven. He causes His sun to rise on the evil and the good, and sends rain on the righteous and the unrighteous. If you love those who love you, what reward will you get? (MATTHEW 5:38-39, 44-46)

This Scripture, and others like it, are interpreted by many Christians as replacing the old way of doing things where fire was fought with fire. The defense would say that Old Testament examples—such as Joshua's campaigns—are no longer valid examples for us to follow, because Christ has ushered in a new age. Michael Ortiz would have been more in line with Christian teaching if he had waged a war of prayer and forgiveness against the drug smugglers.

BRINGING IT HOME: THE APPLICATION

Many of you could be considering careers in fields where you might be asked to sometimes go against your personal convictions to serve a higher purpose. In some occupations, such as police work or the armed services, that's more clearly seen. But have you ever thought about the ethical problems you might run into in other fields—teaching, law, or medicine, for example? Consider:

- the teacher who must expel a disruptive student so the rest of the class can continue to learn.
- the attorney who defends a client she knows is guilty because that person is entitled by law to a defense.
- the medical doctor who gives out birth-control pills to a sexually active teenage girl so she won't bring an unwanted child into the world.

In these situations you might feel pressured to do

something you find distasteful—even immoral—so that a greater good will be served. In these instances the "greater good" includes education of the group, the right of every person to have a competent defense in court, and the prevention of teenage pregnancy.

As a teacher, attorney, or doctor, what would be your personal response to such conflicting choices? It will be helpful *before* the situation arises to spend some time thinking about possible conflicts of interest and ethical problems which might occur in the career you are considering, and decide ahead of time, if possible, what choices you will make.

The issue of the end justifying the means will also present itself on a smaller scale in your life, if it hasn't already. For example, sometimes a Christian will date a non-Christian, saying that this is a good way to witness because the non-Christian will be able to see Christ in the other's life. Or a Christian might not hesitate to tell a little white lie in order to spare someone's feelings or protect his or her reputation. Some Christians will go to a party and join in the drinking because they don't want people to think that Christians are always "straitlaced" and no fun.

There is a point where our careful reasoning in these "gray" areas breaks down and becomes simply an excuse for wrongdoing. Think about the situations above, or similar ones in your own life. Do you see a border line that should not be crossed?

THE APPEAL: REOPENING THE CASE

Now go back and reread the "Case of the Devastated Detective" at the beginning of this chapter. Once again, give your verdict and the reasoning behind your decision.

Do you find for the:

THE CASE OF THE DEVASTATED DETECTIVE

☐ Prosecution?
☐ Defense?
Why?

Did your decision change? Did your reasoning?

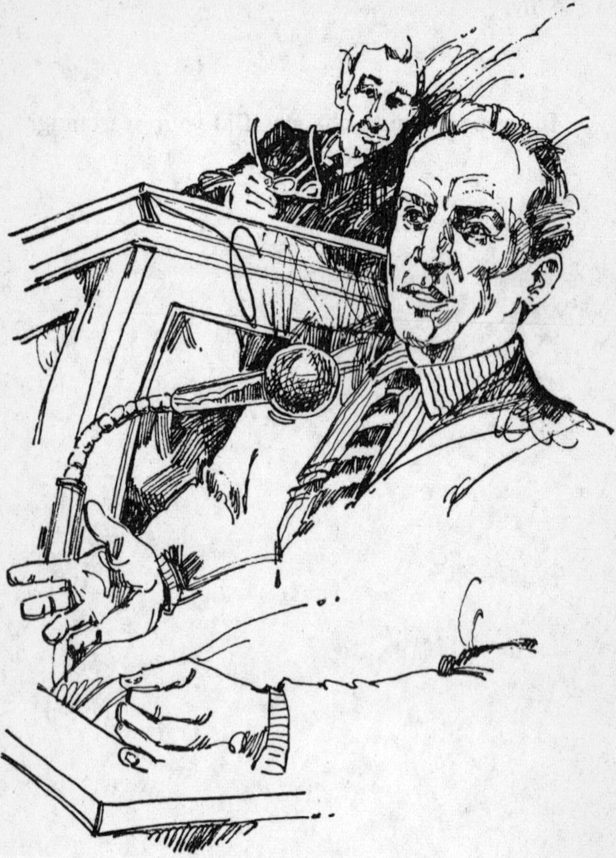

4. THE CASE OF THE FAMILY FEUD

THE FACTS OF THE CASE

Heidi McVay couldn't understand why her father was making such a big deal out of it.

"OK, kids, this is it," he had said as he pulled a stack of travel brochures out of his briefcase and scattered them on the dining room table. "The chance of a lifetime. This year I get three weeks paid vacation, and for once I'm actually going to take them! This is one trip that won't get canceled because of some problem at the plant." With that he proceeded to explain that the family was going to take a grand tour of the New England states to make up for all the times they had to stay home because of Mr. McVay's job.

"It's going to be great! We'll be spending a lot of time together; we'll be a real family. I realize this is probably the last chance we'll have to take a trip together before you kids start working summer jobs and going off on your own, so just count on a good time!"

The trip looked like everything her dad said it would be, but Heidi had other plans. She told her father that she was sorry, but she just couldn't go along. She reminded him that she was going to take part in a summer mission project in the inner city helping teach disadvantaged kids who were behind in school and conducting neighborhood Bible studies with them. Operation Teach had been planned for many months, and Heidi was in charge. Since two other volunteers had already dropped out, it was terribly important that she follow through with her commitment.

"Nothing doing," said Mr. McVay. "Your family is more important than a bunch of kids that you don't even know. You're a member of this family, and you're going with us."

"But Dad," pleaded Heidi, "it's just a vacation. Operation Teach is more important than a *vacation!*"

"Not when your family is involved, it isn't. Look, young lady, we've all put up with a lot from you. You spend plenty of time away from home with all this church stuff. I'm your father, you're my seventeen-year-old daughter, and the discussion ends right now. You're going on vacation with your family."

Desperate, Heidi made an appointment to see her pastor. She explained her problem: how her family was not Christian and had never understood her convictions, how she felt that God's will was for her to work with Operation Teach, how unfair she thought it was for her father to impose his wishes on her and force her to give up her own plans.

"I know it's tough, Heidi," said her pastor, "but your father is right. As the head of your family, God has put him in authority over you. While you're still a 'child,' your duty is to obey him."

"He's not even a Christian!"

"That doesn't matter. He's still your father, and you must do as he says."

Against her personal convictions, Heidi reported

THE CASE OF THE FAMILY FEUD

back to her family that she had quit Operation Teach and would be going on the family vacation. Once she made that decision, she tried to be happy and was actually looking forward to the trip.

Operation Teach was canceled because Heidi was unable to find her own replacement, and without her there were just too few workers.

CHARGES: Heidi's pastor is accused of giving out ill-considered advice and putting God's will second to Heidi's dad's wishes.

THE ARGUMENTS

PROSECUTION: The guilty party in the "Case of the Family Feud" is not really Heidi McVay, even though her decision to quit Operation Teach resulted in a lost opportunity to reach people for God. Are we saying Heidi is free of blame simply because of her youth? No. She *is* responsible for her actions in this case. But the *real* fault lies with her pastor who wrongly advised her to place her father's wishes over the will of God.

Even though Heidi made it clear that she felt it was God's will to work with Operation Teach that summer, her pastor failed to honor her call, advising instead that she fulfill a family obligation. As a result, her father, a non-Christian, was placed in a position to judge spiritual matters. His role as father did not qualify him to be the final authority in this situation.

Heidi McVay's pastor, her trusted spiritual adviser, failed to give her thoughtful, prayerful counsel. He is guilty of putting the wishes of Heidi's father ahead of God's will.

DEFENSE: Heidi McVay and her pastor wisely decided to obey God by working within the framework of authority and submission that He Himself established. From the beginning of time we see God putting one person over another because without leadership there is confusion and disorder.

This is not to say that authority is always easy to follow or that those in leadership positions are always wise and fair. But the fact remains that in God's plan parents are put in charge of their children to do what they think best. Children must obey their parents out of reverence for God—regardless of whether or not the child can immediately see the logic of the parents' reasoning.

When Mr. McVay said that Heidi was to go with the family on vacation, Heidi was right to agree even though her father is a non-Christian. Similarly, she must obey civil laws—stopping at a red light, for example—even though traffic laws are not necessarily set by Christians. It is not our place to question authority at every turn, but simply to obey.

Heidi's goal in this situation should have been to present a strong example to her family of Christlike love and submission. It is sometimes tempting to show more concern for nameless others than for our own family and friends. There are any number of qualified people who can work with programs like Operation Teach, but Heidi may be the only one who can bring the Gospel to her family.

Heidi's pastor did the right thing in upholding God's plan for order on earth. We can find no fault with his actions.

YOU BE THE JUDGE

What is your verdict? Do you find for the:
- ☐ Prosecution?
- ☐ Defense?

THE CASE OF THE FAMILY FEUD

Why? Explain your reasoning.

CASE BACKGROUND

The question of moral responsibility is an important one in this case. Should Heidi be held accountable for her decision, even though at the age of seventeen she is legally a minor and under her parents' control? We might begin to explore that question by drawing a line between "youth" and "adult."

There are many different definitions of youth. We generally think of it as a time when a child is under his parents' care and depending on their financial support. In the United States, a sixteen-year-old can assume some adult responsibilities—such as driving a car or quitting school if he chooses. At the age of eighteen he can marry without parental consent, vote in federal elections, and in many states sign legal contracts and purchase alcoholic beverages. These rights and privileges reflect our culture's thinking on youth and adulthood.

Jews and Christians believe the age of twelve is the "age of accountability." That is the time when an individual is mature enough to decide for himself how he will respond to God. It marks the end of innocence and the beginning of responsibility.

Young people *have* done amazing things. Joan of Arc was indeed martyred for her faith at the age of nineteen. Joash was seven years old when he began his reign as king of Jerusalem; Josiah was only eight. Samuel clearly heard God's call at an early age (1 SAMUEL 3).

Timothy was a young pastor who received advice from the Apostle Paul about his youth:

> *Don't let anyone look down on you because you are young, but set an example for the believers in*

speech, in life, in love, in faith and in purity. Do not neglect your gift, which was given you through a prophetic message when the body of elders laid their hands on you (1 TIMOTHY 4:12, 14).

Though Scripture provides few glimpses into the early life of Christ, we do know that He conversed with the temple rabbis as a boy, probably at the age of twelve.

SOME LEAD; OTHERS FOLLOW

We can turn to God's Word for background on another issue tied to this case—the question of authority. In Scripture we see God's plan that some are meant to lead, while others must follow. As early as the first chapter of Genesis the plan develops:

God blessed them and said to them, "Be fruitful and increase in number; fill the earth and subdue it. Rule over the fish of the sea and the birds of the air and over every living creature that moves on the ground" (GENESIS 1:28).

Later, God directed Moses to choose leaders who would have the power to judge disputes and command troops (DEUTERONOMY 1:9-18). This chain of command was set up mainly to save time so Moses wouldn't have to be bothered with every decision himself.

Through the years, governments have changed. But the principles given to God's people remain the same.

Everyone must submit himself to the governing authorities, for there is no authority except that which God has established. The authorities that exist have been established by God. Consequently, he who rebels against the authority is

THE CASE OF THE FAMILY FEUD 51

rebelling against what God has instituted, and those who do so will bring judgment on themselves (ROMANS 13:1-2).

Submit yourselves for the Lord's sake to every authority instituted among men: whether to the king, as the supreme authority, or to governors, who are sent by him to punish those who do wrong and to commend those who do right. For it is God's will that by doing good you should silence the ignorant talk of foolish men (1 PETER 2:13-15).

These instructions to obey authority were written during a time of harsh Roman laws. Still, Christians were told to obey the ruling powers.

A TIME TO DISOBEY

What does all this have to do with Heidi McVay going on vacation with her parents? As a minor child, Heidi must confront the same issues in her relationship to her parents that all Christians face in relating to civil (non-Christian) authorities. There *is* a time for children to disobey their parents, just as there are sometimes good reasons for disobeying civil authorities.

For example, in 1 Samuel 19:1-6 we see that Jonathan was ordered by his father, Saul, to kill David. Jonathan went against Saul's wishes and even talked his father into letting David live. Later, when Saul decided again that David should die, Jonathan defied his father and warned David to escape (1 SAMUEL 20).

Returning to the story of Jesus teaching in the temple (LUKE 2:41-50), we see a picture of Christ doing His "Father's business" (God's), even though it caused His parents trouble and worry. Still, after the incident was over, Jesus went back to the traditional role of a Jewish child living with his parents:

> *Then He went down to Nazareth with them and was obedient to them. But His mother treasured all these things in her heart. And Jesus grew in wisdom and stature, and in favor with God and men* (LUKE 2:51-52).

Christ taught His followers to uphold the Mosaic Law in the normal parent-child relationship: *"Honor your father and your mother, so that you may live long in the land the Lord your God is giving you"* (EXODUS 20:12). Christ said: *"And why do you break the command of God for the sake of your tradition? For God said, 'Honor your father and mother'"* (MATTHEW 15:3-4).

KEY QUESTIONS

1. Do you suspect that Mr. McVay might be a "workaholic" father who is desperately trying to make up for the mistakes of the last seventeen years?

2. Do you get the idea that Heidi has ignored her family because they aren't Christians? Has she neglected them because she's so involved in her own interests?

3. Should Mr. McVay have let Heidi stay home when he found out that Operation Teach would actually have to be canceled because of her backing out?

4. Did her pastor give enough thought to the fact that Heidi felt it was God's will for her to work with Operation Teach that summer?

5. Does it make a difference that Heidi's father is a non-Christian?

6. How can Heidi make sure that the summer vacation with her family is put to the best possible use?

someone else's wishes ahead of our own, follow the laws of our country, obey traffic laws, and submit to our parents, we are thinking of others more than ourselves. This is no more than Christ did when He lived on earth. He gave up all His rights and privileges to become one of us and *show* us the way of salvation.

When the Bible says that our parents or the civil authorities are God's agents here on earth, we can see that God does work through them in teaching us how to relate to Him. We do not have to believe that those over us are perfectly wise. But by lowering ourselves a notch and following the authority of others, we will learn some practical lessons about our own relationships with God.

BRINGING IT HOME: THE APPLICATION

Every now and then you read a newspaper headline that goes something like this:

PARENTS REFUSE BLOOD TRANSFUSIONS;
STATE SEEKS CUSTODY OF DYING CHILD

or

TEENAGER SUES PARENTS FOR NEGLECT
"THEY WOULDN'T PAY FOR PROM"

or

BIRTH-CONTROL CLINIC PROTECTS
PRIVACY RIGHTS OF TEENAGE CLIENTS

These headlines all point to one of the major questions in this case: At what point does a parent's authority end and a young person's right to decide begin? It's a question you could easily ask yourself when you come up against a big disagreement with your own parents.

Parent-child relationships are changing rapidly these days. Sometimes it isn't clear what a parent's rights and responsibilities really are. Many parents feel that society and the government are taking away their God-given authority over their own children.

Have you ever been in Heidi McVay's situation? Have you thought that you were right and your parents were wrong, but you had to go along with them anyway just because they were your parents? Do your political and religious opinions get ignored at your house because "you're just a kid"? Do you have to change your own plans because your parents have volunteered you for visiting relatives, baby-sitting younger brothers or sisters, or doing chores? Do you come from a non-Christian home where your faith is laughed at or put down?

It is challenging to be a part of a family—for your parents as well as for you. Families are important; they help hold society together. But there are times when other things are *more* important than family relationships. Christ said:

> *Do not suppose that I have come to bring peace to the earth. I did not come to bring peace, but a sword. For I have come to turn "a man against his father, a daughter against her mother, a daughter-in-law against her mother-in-law—a man's enemies will be the members of his own household." Anyone who loves his father or mother more than Me is not worthy of Me; anyone who loves his son or daughter more than Me is not worthy of Me* (MATTHEW 10:34-37).

Fighting words? The kiss of death for the family? No. Christ spoke this way so that we would understand clearly where our final loyalty must lie. We are to love

THE CASE OF THE FAMILY FEUD

our families, but we must love God more. When all is said and done, we belong to God, and it is He who must be obeyed first in everything we do.

THE APPEAL: REOPENING THE CASE

Now go back and reread the "Case of the Family Feud" at the beginning of this chapter. Once again, give your verdict and the reasoning behind your decision:

Do you find for the:
☐ Prosecution?
☐ Defense?
Why?

Did your decision change? Did your reasoning?

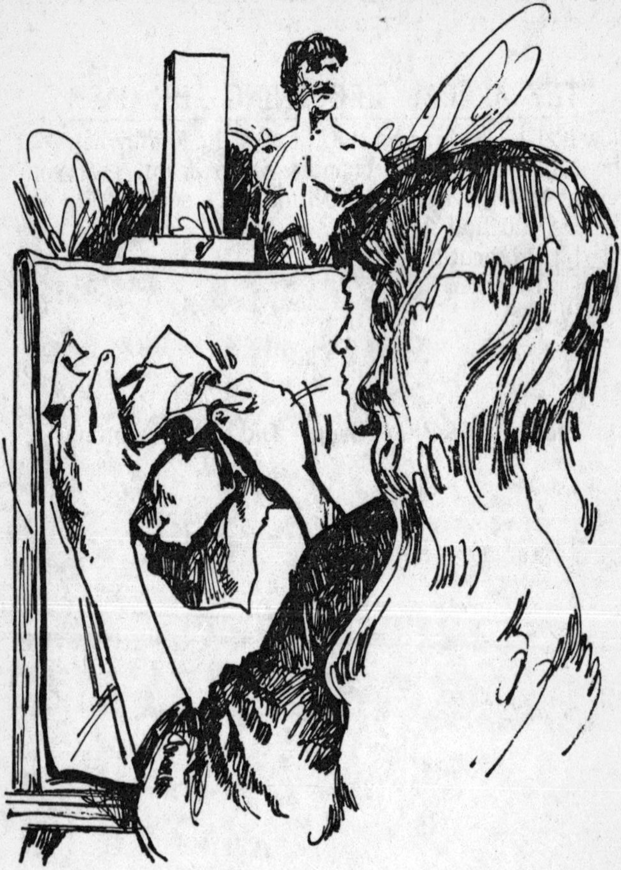

5. THE CASE OF THE IMMODEST MODEL

THE FACTS OF THE CASE

Monica Rogers had excelled in art ever since she was a little girl. She couldn't have been more excited when she got the news that she could attend the Midwest Art Institute. With its first-rate facilities and talented teachers, M.A.I. accepted only the finest young artists. A diploma from the school would help her launch a bright career as a free-lance artist.

But even before she started taking classes, Monica was bothered by one thing. She knew that several classes used nude models for drawing, painting, and sculpting. One of them, "Drawing from Life," was a requirement for graduation. As a Christian, Monica felt uneasy about the idea and wondered if it would be right to take part in the class.

The semesters passed and Monica became wrapped up in her work at the Institute, pushing the problem of "Drawing from Life" to the back of her mind. But, during her sophomore year, her adviser called her in for a conference.

"Monica, you still have one requirement to take care of—'Drawing from Life.'"

Monica said nothing, but her face reddened in reply.

"I understand that some students have a hard time thinking about drawing nudes, but we all do it, my Dear. You'll get over it."

Still Monica didn't speak. What could she say to her adviser about the way she had been raised, her belief in the importance of sexual purity, her religious convictions?

"I'll go ahead and put it on your schedule for next semester. Really, it'll be OK!" said the bemused adviser as Monica rose and walked out of the office.

Monica's feelings of confusion and guilt became stronger and stronger. She didn't dare tell her parents about her problem. If they knew drawing from nudes was a part of the curriculum, they would be so shocked they'd probably pull her out of school. None of her classmates seemed to share her concern. There were a few jokes about the class, but everyone agreed that drawing from nudes is an important part of any good art education.

When Monica attended the first class session, the details of the course were given. Former art students and members of the community—both male and female—would be posing. Students would be required to submit sixteen studies of the models and four finished pen-and-ink drawings. They would help evaluate each other's work and had to read and be tested on an anatomy text. The final grade would be based on understanding and expression of the human form.

At the second class session, drawing began. The model turned out to be a young man who worked on the Institute's maintenance staff. With the other students, Monica began her sketch. The first ten minutes or so were almost unbearably embarrassing for her, but she

THE CASE OF THE IMMODEST MODEL

tried to overcome her shyness by concentrating on her work. After several trashed beginnings she became totally absorbed in what she was doing. By the end of the hour she had produced a pencil drawing that she was very pleased with.

As the weeks passed, Monica became fascinated by her work and spent nearly all her free time reading additional books, studying life drawings and paintings at the Civic Art Gallery, and filling her sketchbooks with drawings of the human body.

At the close of the semester she was enjoying this class more than any other she was taking and had already signed up for "Sculpting from Life."

CHARGES: Monica is accused of participating in sexual immorality, which is condemned time and time again in the Bible.

THE ARGUMENTS

PROSECUTION: Monica knew well in advance what would be demanded of her if she attended the Midwest Art Institute. She might have gone to any number of other good schools that did not have this requirement, or she might have tried to get out of taking the class entirely. But she did not even speak out against the nudity when she had the chance. Instead, she merely turned red and let her adviser talk her into the class.

The real issue here, though, is that Monica believed the lie that anything goes as long as you call it "art." This simply is not true. We must not make the mistake of letting a label make something sinful seem acceptable. Public nudity is immodest, immoral, and totally out of God's will. Art is not free from this standard, no matter how you try to justify it. The Bible clearly states that such displays are unacceptable, and that is reason enough to refuse to draw from a nude model.

While it may be possible to draw from a nude model without arousing feelings of lust in the artist or model, that is not likely the case in a sophomore art class where a group of late-adolescents are ogling the campus maintenance man, recording his likeness on paper, and then discussing it afterward!

As the semester progresses, we see Monica "freed" from her earlier feelings of guilt about the class. This shows clearly how exposure to immorality deadens our senses so that we eventually come to accept our sins merely because we have practiced them for so long.

To make matters worse, Monica contributed to the downfall of the immodest model, who would not be posing nude if there was no call for his services. Her actions caused the model to break God's laws. As an informed Christian Monica must accept responsibility for his actions as well as her own.

The art class becomes, at this point, an example of society's moral breakdown. What's next? A class in "Photographing the Nude"? Should we look for the names of Christians on the mastheads of *Playboy* and *Penthouse?* Enough is enough. If Christian young people will not oppose such open disrespect for the Bible's teachings, who will?

DEFENSE: It is as morally acceptable for a serious art student to sketch from a live model as it is for a medical student to practice his or her skills on real patients.

We must not confuse sexual immorality with nudity. No "sin of the flesh" takes place when the human form, as God created it, is studied with the purpose of being able to represent it through art. From a purely practical point of view the artist can no more be expected to draw a true likeness of a body she has never seen than a

THE CASE OF THE IMMODEST MODEL

doctor can be expected to prescribe proper treatment without a physical examination of the patient.

Monica did the right thing. She overcame her shyness and took part in the class. By doing do, she discovered that the human body is the most fascinating of all art subjects, the most worthy of interpretation and expression. Through the ages, artists have realized this. Michelangelo's "David," Botticelli's "Birth of Venus," and Lucas Cranach's "Adam and Eve" are but a few examples of the use of nudity by Christian artists.

Nudity in art is not pornography. Pornography is the exhibition of sexual material for the purpose of causing arousal and excitement. By its very nature pornography is degrading and exploitive. Nudity in art represents something normal and natural—our bodies, which God created.

No wonder Monica Rodgers became wrapped up in her work as the semester went on. Once she began her sketching, she realized that what she was doing was not wrong and did not break God's moral law. Through her art, Monica could celebrate the body that God created and share in the artistic tradition of the centuries.

YOU BE THE JUDGE

What is your verdict? Do you find for the:
- [ ] Prosecution?
- [ ] Defense?

Why? Explain your reasoning.

CASE BACKGROUND

In the beginning, we are told that clothes were not worn in the Garden of Eden. *"The man and his wife were both naked, and they felt no shame"* (GENESIS 2:25). After the fall of Adam and Eve, the situation changed. *"The eyes of both of them were opened, and they realized they were naked; so they sewed fig leaves together and made coverings for themselves"* (GENESIS 3:7).

From these Scriptures it is apparent that shame in nakedness arose out of man's Fall and his resulting disfavor with God. When there was no sin in the world, man was innocent and didn't care about clothing. After he rebelliously chose to know good and evil, he was quick to cover himself.

Later in the Old Testament is the story of David and Bathsheba (2 SAMUEL 11). David saw Bathsheba bathing—naked, we can presume—and this excited such lust in him that he committed adultery with her and planned the death of her husband so he could have her for his wife.

David would have done well to set for himself the higher standard of Christ, who said:

> *You have heard that it was said, "Do not commit adultery." But I tell you that anyone who looks at a woman lustfully has already committed adultery with her in his heart. If your right eye causes you to sin, gouge it out and throw it away. It is better for you to lose one part of your body than for your whole body to be thrown into hell* (MATTHEW 5:27-29).

This Scripture is the Prosecution's keystone, as the prosecution claims it would be almost impossible for Monica Rodgers to draw a nude man without having feelings of lust, feelings which could lead to other sins. No one is asking the student to gouge her eyes out, but she could avoid temptation in this case by not attending the life-drawing class.

MODESTY IS THE BEST POLICY

The Bible also speaks to the issue of modesty, even though standards of modest dress and behavior have changed since Bible times. The defense would argue that while biblical attitudes of modesty still apply to us today, we no longer follow the specific instructions given Christians of an earlier day.

For example, the Apostle Paul wrote:

> *Judge for yourselves: Is it proper for a woman to pray to God with her head uncovered? Does not the very nature of things teach you that if a man has long hair, it is a disgrace to him, but that if a woman has long hair, it is her glory? For long hair is given to her as a covering. If anyone wants to be contentious about this, we have no other practice—nor do the churches of God* (1 CORINTHIANS 11:13-16).

In this passage, we can see that the first readers—members of the church at Corinth—understood exactly what Paul was saying and why he was saying it. Phrases such as "Does not the very nature of things teach you" and "We have no other practice" imply that his audience knew what was proper and improper in worship.

Reading the passage today, though, we are confused. For one thing, what length is "long" hair and why is it a disgrace? And how does long hair on a woman provide "a covering"? What would Paul think if he saw average churchgoers on Sunday morning—a wide variety of hair lengths, women with knee-length skirts and sleeveless dresses? Would trousers (unknown in Bible times) be considered proper attire for worship? Because standards of dress have changed, it is difficult to get clear advice on what is proper for a Christian in today's culture and in Monica's circumstances.

KEY QUESTIONS

The defense is not in favor of sexual immorality, nor is the prosecution against art. But the defense does not think nudity is sexually immoral, and the prosecution does not believe that nudity is art. Both have argued well from these positions. To help you reach a decision, let's consider some practical questions related to the issues brought out in this case.

1. At the end of the "Case of the Immodest Model" we see Monica Rodgers—for one reason or another—no longer troubled by sketching from a nude model. What do you think changed her attitude?

2. Could an art student learn as much about the human form by drawing from a model who was clothed in a swimming suit, body stocking, or leotard?

3. Is it right to compare Monica Rodgers to a medical student? Is modesty less of an issue between a doctor and patient than it is in the world of art?

4. What about the models? Monica Rodgers was eventually comfortable drawing a model. Should she have been willing to pose herself? Or is that something else altogether? Is she responsible for the model's actions by taking part in the class?

5. Is there a difference between an art student at a respected art academy drawing from a live model and a student in a high school art class doing the same? Why or why not?

6. The prosecution mentioned a class in "Photographing the Nude." Do you think there is a difference between a painting of a nude and a photograph of a nude? Would such a course have a place in a Christian's art training?

7. What about the famous works of art that depict nudes? Take Michelangelo's "David" for example. It is an imposing marble sculpture of a nude David with his slingshot. Surely David was not naked when he killed

THE CASE OF THE IMMODEST MODEL

Goliath. Why did Michelangelo portray him without clothes? Is this what we would call "gratuitous sex" today?

8. Can you think of other ways that Monica Rodgers might have handled this situation?

As usual these key questions help pinpoint our attitudes about the "gray areas" in this case. For instance, we might come to the conclusion that it is all right for Monica to draw from a nude model. But when we ask if she should pose herself, we have doubts again. We might be comfortable browsing through an art gallery where classic paintings of nudes are displayed beside landscapes and portraits. When the same gallery has an exhibit of nude photographs, we question the good taste of such a showing.

THE FINAL ANALYSIS

Let's dig deeper into the main issue in this case—modesty. What *is* modesty? In the Bible modesty often means the same thing as humility. The dictionary defines *modesty* as "being proper in dress and behavior" as well as "freedom from conceit or vanity." *Humility* is to be "not proud or arrogant; reflecting a spirit of submission." When modesty touches on how we dress, it is easy to see that a lack of what we consider modesty (wearing skimpy bathing suits or tight and revealing clothing) often occurs when we are trying to be noticed and admired. At this point we also lack humility because we want to make ourselves the center of attention when we should be putting others first.

The same holds true with *over*dressing. Paul says, *"I also want women to dress modestly, with decency and propriety, not with braided hair or gold or pearls or expensive clothes"* (1 TIMOTHY 2:9).

Some Christians dress to the hilt on a Sunday morning—fur coat, jewels, expensive suits—to show respect for God in worship. But others believe plain clothes are a sign of humility and respect for God and their fellow worshipers.

If modesty in dress is a sign of our inward humility, how does that affect the "Case of the Immodest Model"? We must ask ourselves if Monica Rodgers, her classmates, teachers, and the models are trying to call attention to themselves, their appearance, and skills, or if they are really acting out of humble appreciation for God's creation—the human body.

BRINGING IT HOME: THE APPLICATION

You will probably never be faced with Monica Rodgers' problem. However, you do have to deal with our culture's changing standards of dress and behavior.

Did you decide that it would have been OK for the art students to draw from a model wearing a leotard or bodystocking? You probably did. But even fifty years ago that would have raised eyebrows. Do you remember the old-fashioned bathing suits: tank top and knee-length bottoms for men and bloomers with short-sleeved blouses for women? Those one-piece suits caused a real uproar when people started showing up on the beach in them.

More recently, there have been furors over long hair on men, short skirts on women, see-through blouses, short-shorts, bikinis. . . . The list goes on and on. Often Christians who are at first set against the newer looks come to accept them as they become less associated with rebellion and are worn by a larger segment of the population.

Look around at clothes your friends are wearing

THE CASE OF THE IMMODEST MODEL

right now. Can you imagine them showing up for a church meeting at the turn of the century dressed like that? Probably no one would be allowed through the doors looking as they do now, including your parents!

Does this mean that Christians have no standards of behavior and dress to follow? Absolutely not! It means that these standards are generally not based on absolutes of what is right and wrong but change according to the attitudes and tastes of society.

We must decide—for ourselves and as a group of Christians—what behavior is modest and what is immodest and displeasing to God. And we must decide when modesty becomes prudery; that is, when it's been carried too far and blown out of proportion. We should judge for ourselves when modesty becomes an end unto itself and not a sign of our humility and respect toward God and our fellowman.

THE APPEAL: REOPENING THE CASE

Now go back and reread the "Case of the Immodest Model" at the beginning of this chapter. Once again, give your verdict and the reasoning behind your decision.

Do you find for the:
☐ Prosecution?
☐ Defense?
Why?

Did your decision change? Did your reasoning?

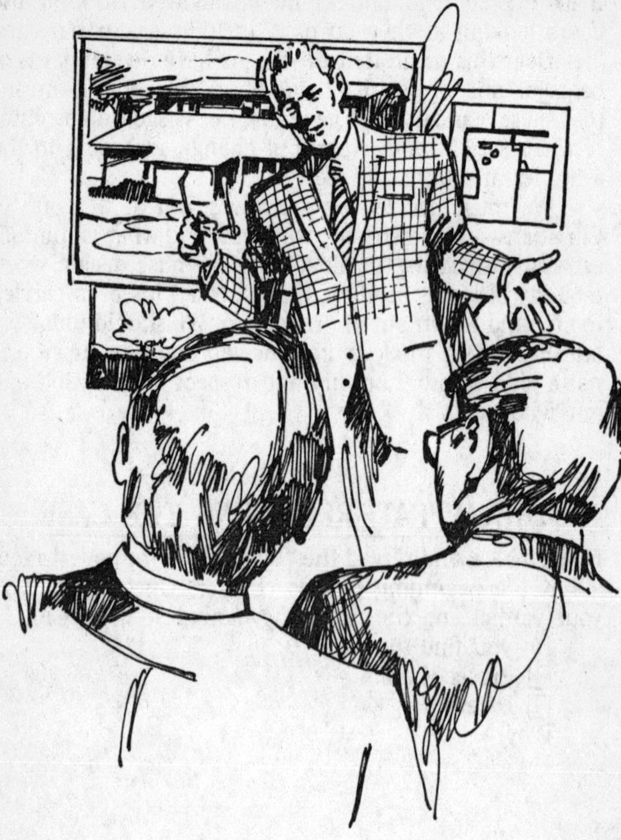

6. THE CASE OF THE DISSENTING DEACON

THE FACTS OF THE CASE

"It is a bold, farseeing, and exciting plan," said the pastor of Oak Hollow Community Church. "The committee has done a wonderful job." He smiled at the colored sketches tacked to the bulletin board behind him.

The Special Committee on Church Growth had just given their final report to the Board of Deacons. The report strongly recommended that the church build a new Family Life Center: a large, well-equipped complex that would include a swimming pool, racquetball courts, jogging track, gymnasium, and educational space.

"These centers are becoming very popular," explained the committee chairman. "Church members get an opportunity to participate in recreational programs as a family. These facilities also have a strong influence on families outside the church. Why, one church in Los Angeles doubled its membership in three years, after building a center."

Roger Erickson, a church deacon and long-time member, was the only one who questioned the project.

"Why do we want to build a Family Life Center?" he asked. "Is it because we have prayed about it and feel led of God to expand our ministry in this way? Or is it because it will give our church status, because building programs give us something to rally around, because we want a tax-deductible health club?"

The others frowned, but Roger continued. "I believe that our current building is large enough for a church our size. Our growth from this Family Life Center would most likely come from stealing people away from other churches—just because we have a more attractive facility. What we need to do here is get our priorities straight. If we have over a million dollars in this congregation to spend, then let's spend it on the aged in our nursing homes or the people in our community who don't have proper food to eat or clothes to wear. Let's raise a million dollars to build a medical clinic for one of our missionaries or help resettle refugees. Let's look beyond our own front door and see where our resources will do the most good."

But very few people, if any, felt as Roger did. And when the project came to a final vote, he was the only one who opposed it. In the meantime, he had made many people uncomfortable with his open criticism of a project they supported wholeheartedly.

As the congregation became more and more involved in building the Family Life Center, Roger had less and less in common with his fellow members. He still believed the others were going in the wrong direction and were doing something in the name of God which only served themselves. As he looked ahead to the coming years when nearly every church-related activity would revolve around the Family Life Center, he felt he had nothing in common with these people who had lost sight of basic Christian principles.

On the day of the ground-breaking for the Family

THE CASE OF THE DISSENTING DEACON

Life Center, Roger Erickson formally submitted his resignation as Deacon of Oak Hollow Community Church and withdrew his membership as well.

CHARGES: Roger Erickson is accused of putting his own concerns above the good of the whole congregation and creating disunity among members of Christ's body.

THE ARGUMENTS

PROSECUTION: If Roger Erickson is looking for a local church where there are no disagreements, no differences of opinion, no conflicts—we can only guarantee he won't find it. In this case he is guilty of sacrificing Christian unity for a stubborn insistence on his own point of view.

Whether or not the Oak Hollow Community Church should or should not build a Family Life Center is really beside the point. We question whether this issue is so important that it is worth a division in the church of Christ. If the dispute were whether Christ is or is not the Son of God, then we might reasonably expect a church split. But a split because of a disagreement over a building program? Surely not!

The thinking and actions of Roger Erickson are just the sort of thing that have weakened the church through the ages. Even though they agree on major doctrines, hundreds of denominations and churches in this country pride themselves on having nothing to do with other Christian groups because they differ on style of worship, method of baptism, how often communion is observed, the role of women, or some minor point of theology. Doesn't anyone value tolerance within the Christian community anymore?

It is a sad thing to see an argument over church programs destroy fellowship of believers. Roger Erickson should have stayed with his church whether or not he could bring himself to their way of thinking. In any case, by reaching a compromise he would be accomplishing more than he did by leaving in a huff because he didn't get his own way.

Of course, the church members are not perfect. It is entirely possible that their Family Life Center is a bad idea and that they have questionable motives for building it. But Roger Erickson is not perfect either, and one must wonder what *his* motives are in leaving his church over such a minor issue. He could have demonstrated his commitment to the body. He could have learned something about understanding and forgiveness. Instead of trying, he just packed up and moved out.

DEFENSE: It is absurd to call stewardship a *minor* issue. It is an issue of *major* importance, and Roger Erickson had every right and responsibility to speak out. When his warnings continued to fall on deaf ears, it was time for him to leave.

Where would Christianity be today if men of faith had not spoken out against hypocrisy and false teaching in the organized church? Could Martin Luther be called a troublemaker and rebel for leaving the Catholic church? Are John Calvin, John Wesley, and other reformers to be criticized now because they had calls and visions that were not recognized by the church of their day?

A large group of people can often get swept away in excitement and act in a way that is no longer consistent with God's leading. Each believer must not be swayed by the group, but must instead seek to know God's will in deciding what to do.

Christian unity is a goal we must strive for, but it is never more important than our own relationship to God. Unity is never more important than matters of right and wrong. When a group of Christians are no

THE CASE OF THE DISSENTING DEACON

longer in tune with an individual's Christian convictions, then it is time for the individual to leave and find fellowship with more like-minded brothers.

YOU BE THE JUDGE

What is your verdict? Do you find for the:
☐ Prosecution?
☐ Defense?
Why? Explain your reasoning.

CASE BACKGROUND

I appeal to you, brothers, in the name of our Lord Jesus Christ, that all of you agree with one another so that there may be no divisions among you and that you may be perfectly united in mind and thought (1 CORINTHIANS 1:10).

Unity seems an impossible dream for the Christian church. Throughout the ages the church has experienced disagreements, controversy, factions, and splits.

In the third century after the death of Christ there was a movement away from the established church of that day. Those who left were called monks. They turned their backs on society and a corrupt, materialistic church to live a life of prayer and poverty.

A Catholic monk named Martin Luther first challenged the sixteenth-century church over a financial matter: the selling of indulgences (forgiveness) by the priests. There was no room for disagreement in the church of Luther's day, and he was expelled. Alrich Swingli and Menno Simons (on whose teachings the Mennonite church was formed) along with John Calvin were viewed as troublemakers when their convictions caused them to reject the established church.

Still, there were some reformors who were able to stay within the church—St. Francis of Assisi, Ignatius Loyola, and others. But most reformers eventually sided with other "*Protest*ants."

John Wesley, the founder of the Methodist church, was a missionary of the Church of England. At first he planned to stay with the established order but, again, there was a lack of compromise on both sides and another denomination was born. Other groups such as the Baptists, Quakers, Shakers, and Dutch Reformed also opted to draw away from their original fellowships and set up their own churches which followed their strongest beliefs.

In Scripture the church is often called the body of Christ. A body, though made of many parts, must be able to work as a whole, as these Scriptures direct:

Finally, brothers, good-bye. Aim for perfection, listen to my appeal, be of one mind, live in peace. And the God of love and peace will be with you (2 CORINTHIANS 13:11).

Whatever happens, conduct yourselves in a manner worthy of the Gospel of Christ. Then, whether I come and see you or only hear about you in my absence, I will know that you stand firm in one spirit, contending as one man for the faith of the Gospel (PHILIPPIANS 1:27).

Finally, all of you, live in harmony with one another; be sympathetic, love as brothers, be compassionate and humble (1 PETER 3:8).

The community of faith is instructed to live in uni-

THE CASE OF THE DISSENTING DEACON

ty, even in the midst of disagreement. Does that mean there is no basis for leaving a group which calls itself Christian, yet behaves contrary to God's will?

The defense would argue that historical splits in the church—though sometimes painful and difficult—are often a renewing force in Christianity. These splits purify the church, call it into account, and allow God to move more freely in the lives of individual Christians.

The defense also has Scripture which backs up its claim that one must not cooperate with those who no longer obey God. The Apostle Paul writes:

> *See to it that no one takes you captive through hollow and deceptive philosophy, which depends on human tradition and the basic principles of this world rather than on Christ* (COLOSSIANS 2:8).

Again comparing the church to the body of Christ, the defense would say that a part of the body can become sick and that it is up to the healthy parts to do something about the sickness. In the "Case of the Dissenting Deacon," Roger Erickson decided to remove himself from a "sick" congregation and make his own stand for what he believed to be right and in God's will.

KEY QUESTIONS

We have talked so far about division within the church, and church splits. But in the "Case of the Dissenting Deacon," all we really have is one man who leaves his congregation. Is that a church split?

No, it's not a split, but it does have the characteristics of a split: people divided over opinions and the hard feelings of broken friendships.

So, for purposes of deciding whether or not Roger Erickson did the right thing in leaving the church, let's raise some questions related to church divisions.

1. Does the fact that Roger Erickson was the only member against the Family Life Center make his opinion seem less valid? Do you believe that the majority is usually right?

2. Could Roger have voiced his opposition without alienating his friends and fellow members? If he hadn't made so many enemies with his criticism, would it have been easier for him to stay?

3. Make a list of some matters *you* think members of a church must agree on. For example, is it important that every member believe in the same method of baptism or hold the same view of the inspiration of Scripture?

4. The defense seems to be saying that Roger Erickson may have some of the qualities of a modern-day prophet, or reformer. What do you think?

5. Has the Christian church been strengthened or weakened by disagreements and divisions through the years? Is it better to compromise some beliefs for the sake of unity, or is it better to take a stand against questionable teaching and behavior?

6. Do some research on your own church. Is it part of a denomination? How did that denomination form? What about your local congregation? Is it the result of a split, or have other congregations split away from it? What issues were involved?

7. What other choices did Roger Erickson have besides withdrawing his membership from the Oak Hollow Community Church?

THE FINAL ANALYSIS

We see that the prosecution and defense have different values. The prosecution values unity among Christians, claiming that few beliefs are so important that Christians

THE CASE OF THE DISSENTING DEACON

should allow division over them. The defense places a higher value on right doctrine and being part of a church that accurately reflects one's personal call and personal priorities. Many large denominations are dealing with these issues today. Some are forgetting past differences to join with groups they feel are basically in line with their own beliefs. Other denominations are being torn apart over political issues, beliefs about the inspiration of the Bible, or how church money is spent. Joining and splitting seems to be a practice of the Christian church that—good or bad—cannot be avoided.

How binding is a church commitment? Suppose that Roger Erickson was not a member of Oak Hollow Community Church, but just a visitor. If he decided, after attending a few services that the congregation wasn't to his liking, no one would have blamed him for taking his search for a church home elsewhere. But once he joins, committing himself to service as a deacon, his rejection of the church means more. Now he's part of the church "family," and we expect his decisions to be carefully thought out and prayerfully made.

Looking back through history, it is apparent that church splits have been both positive and negative. We can see that it was probably good for Martin Luther to pull away from the Catholic church and begin the Protestant Reformation. It is also good that St. Francis of Assisi, despite basic differences, remained committed to the Catholic church and worked within that system. Similarly, Roger Erickson may find a ministry in another church, but he could also still contribute to the work of Oak Hollow Community Church.

BRINGING IT HOME: THE APPLICATION

Throughout your life you will be involved in groups: a political party, a social club, a company you work for, a group of friends, an athletic team, a neighborhood organization. People join themselves together on the basis of a shared interest or because they want to accomplish something that needs the help and support of others. Members of any group have major points of agreement. Group members may also disagree, even violently, on certain points.

Members of a political organization, for example, might disagree on who should get the presidential nomination, whether or not a constitutional amendment should be defeated, or how best to achieve their goals. Still they function as a whole.

Now, there will be some members who never question party judgment and avoid working out the issues for themselves. Others will be unable to stay with the group if *any* disagreement presents itself. Both attitudes are wrong. One type of member loses his identity in the group, and the other type never learns to tolerate another person's opinion.

With your own friends, you must keep your individuality by expressing your personal opinions. At the same time, the welfare of the group must also be taken into account. And it is up to each person to clearly understand where the group ends and the individual begins. It is not always easy to know when to stay with the group and when to go. When the time comes, you must make that decision for yourself. Just try to be sure that you're not simply taking the easy way out or overreacting to a tough situation.

THE APPEAL: REOPENING THE CASE

Now go back and reread the "Case of the Dissenting Deacon" at the beginning of this chapter. Once again, give your verdict and the reasoning behind your decision.

THE CASE OF THE DISSENTING DEACON

Do you find for the:
☐ Prosecution?
☐ Defense?
Why?

Did your decision change? Did your reasoning?

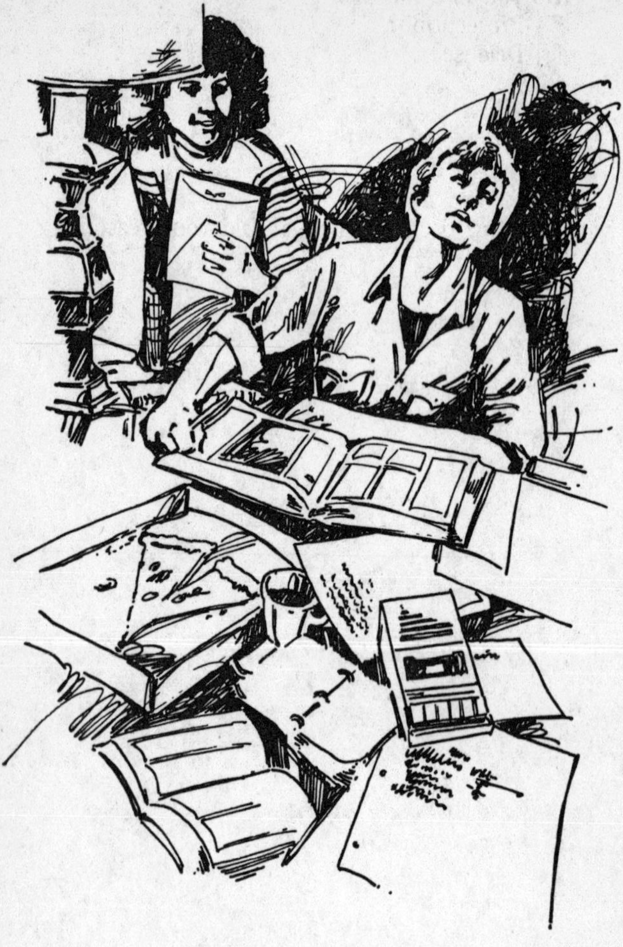

7. THE CASE OF THE FILCHED FINAL

THE FACTS OF THE CASE

Gary Wilson, a third-year student at University Medical School, was studying when Gretchen Shaffer knocked on the door of his room.

"Good news, Gary," she said, holding out a large envelope. "Johnson got hold of Ichenberger's test. This copy's for you."

"Are you serious? That's Friday's exam?"

Gretchen began to remove the envelope's contents to show Gary. He grabbed the envelope from her and pushed the papers back in. "Hey, I don't want to see that!" he said.

"Well, maybe you think you don't need this, Dr. Schweitzer! But you'd better take it. Ichenberger's grading on a curve, and if you don't use this, your grade will go down. Anyway, I've got to go. We're meeting at Rudy's for pizza at 9:00 to compare notes. See you then!"

Gary was left in his room, staring at the brown envelope whose contents could assure him an "A" in histology. He wasn't seriously thinking of opening it; he'd turned down opportunities to cheat before. He knew he could do a good job on the histology final without the stolen test.

But what really bothered him was that Johnson would do something like this. Johnson, Gretchen Shaffer, and three other students were in his study group. They had been together since they were first-year med students and were really close. Three of them were definitely planning to do their residencies at the same hospital and had talked about going into practice together. And now this. Gary was appalled by their dishonesty.

That evening he showed up at Rudy's. "No, I'm not too worried about the histology final," said Morton with a wink. "I think I *know* what to study!" Everyone else chuckled and nodded their heads in agreement.

Gary spoke up. "Look, guys, this is wrong—we shouldn't be doing it."

"Gary," said Johnson, "why do you want to do things the hard way? So you know the material—great. But this test is going to be a killer. Don't be such a Mr. Clean. This is probabaly the biggest break we'll get here. Let's use it."

"No way," Gary said. "I'm not looking at that test, and I don't think you should either."

There was silence around the table while the others exchanged glances.

"Okay, so you've already looked. The damage is done. Let's tell Ichenberger that a copy of his test escaped, and he should make up a new one."

"You're crazy!"

"No, I'm not. Remember—if you get caught cheating you'll be expelled; you'll never practice medicine. I feel real uncomfortable about the fact that I have a copy. That puts me in danger, and I don't like it."

"No one has to know—unless you tell," said

THE CASE OF THE FILCHED FINAL

Gretchen. "Don't do it, Gary."

"To be perfectly honest, I haven't decided."

"Don't be stupid!" said Johnson in a whispered scream. "Look, if we ever get another test we won't involve you. But you have no right to ruin our careers just because you want to study like a fool for no good reason."

"I guess that's my business, isn't it?"

"Sure," said Johnson. "After three years together, it's *your* business. We're your best friends, but it's *your* business. After all we've done for each other, it's *your* business."

Gary left the restaurant and went back to his room to think. An hour later his friends arrived with a question. "What are you going to do, Gary?"

"I'll say this just one more time. You're cheating. It's wrong, and you know it. It's not too late to do the right thing and come clean with Ichenberger. But that's got to come from you. I can't take that responsibility for you."

"Does that mean you won't tell?"

"If anyone finds out about the test, it won't be because of me."

CHARGES: Gary Wilson is accused of cheating on the histology exam since he knew about the crime and did not prevent or expose it.

THE ARGUMENTS

PROSECUTION: By remaining silent about the cheating, Gary deceived everyone connected with the University Medical School: faculty, administration, and students.

The wrongdoing is so clear and unmistakable that we have difficulty understanding how Gary might possibly have justified his silence. Friendship? Certainly not; friends do not ask friends to lie and cheat for them. Loyalty? His real loyalty should be to his Christian principles.

If Gary Wilson cannot accept the fact that he is encouraging dishonesty, then he should at least think about the impact of students cheating on the test. The students who are reviewing the filched final instead of studying will not completely learn the vital information. This gap in their knowledge will affect their ability to grasp other important material and could well make them less competent doctors in the future.

In addition, the students will be "rewarded" for cutting corners and taking the easy way out. They'll find it easier to cheat on other examinations having done so once. And when they are in private practice, they will surely continue the pattern of looking for shortcuts in the treatment of their patients.

Finally, the cheaters hurt their fellow students by throwing off the grading curve. Professor Ichenberger will be figuring grades by rating each student's performance in relation to the entire class. When a handful of students has an unfair advantage over the others (in this case, through seeing the test ahead of time), even those who have studied hard will be unable to reach the artificially high standard.

Gary Wilson's silence has its victims. Clearly, his greatest responsibility is not to his friends, but to the many innocent people who will suffer from his study group's cheating. It is not enough that he didn't look at the filched final himself. He should have reported the theft, regardless of the consequences.

DEFENSE: The prosecution would make a self-righteous do-gooder out of a conscientious Christian. Gary Wilson did the right thing by providing a clear example of moral behavior to his friends. This is all he is

THE CASE OF THE FILCHED FINAL

called to do. It is not his place to police the actions of fellow students or sit in judgment over them.

Gary's role is to be the salt of the earth, to be Christ in the world. Would Christ have reported His friends to the authorities because they broke the law? No, of course not. Did Christ blow the whistle on tax collectors Zaccheus and Matthew because of their cheating? Did He inform on Simon the Zealot to the Romans? No, He established a relationship with them, and the outcome of that relationship was what convicted them of their wrongdoing and changed their lives.

For Gary Wilson to report his friends' actions would only end his relationship with them and cause resentment. Gary is most valuable as a role model, setting a good example for his friends and encouraging ethical behavior. Nothing is gained when he sets himself up in authority over them and takes on a responsibility that is not his. It is not Gary's duty to force others to do right.

The prosecution spoke of the consequences should Gary remain silent about the cheating. Though overstated, they are possible. But the harmful effect of reporting the cheating is certain: personal disgrace, a combined forty years of medical training wasted, and thousands who will be deprived of the care these five students are prepared to offer.

Is it Gary Wilson's responsibility to ruin his friends' futures? Never. He stood up for what was right when it mattered. That alone will have a positive effect and go a long way toward changing his friends' behavior for the better.

YOU BE THE JUDGE

What is your verdict? Do you find for the:
☐ Prosecution?

☐ Defense?
Why? Explain your reasoning.

CASE BACKGROUND

Cheating in this case is a twofold matter—theft of the test and deceit by covering up wrongdoing and pretending to take the test on an equal footing with those who hadn't seen the exam. Leviticus 19:11 pretty well covers the crime of the students, *"Do not steal. Do not lie. Do not deceive one another."*

Christ raised moral standards to a much higher level when He said, *"You have heard that it was said, 'Do not commit adultery.' But I tell you that anyone who looks at a woman lustfully has already committed adultery with her in his heart"* (MATTHEW 5:27-28).

By the same token we must conclude that Gary Wilson's knowledge of his classmates' cheating is in the same category as doing it himself.

The West Point Military Academy code of honor requires cadets to police each others' actions. The code states that a student who knows of cheating, yet fails to report it, is also guilty of cheating and could be expelled. In this case we don't know if the University Medical School has a similar code. We *do* know that if the cheating students are discovered, they will be expelled.

The Bible teaches that the first sin of Adam created an evil nature in mankind that exists to this day. *"Therefore, just as sin entered the world through one man, and death through sin, and in this way death came to all men because all sinned"* (ROMANS 5:12).

There is a communication between one sinful act and another; little deceits have a way of becoming major deceptions. Christians are advised to be honest in everything they do. We never know what negative results

THE CASE OF THE FILCHED FINAL

may come from even small acts of dishonesty.

But what of Gary Wilson's responsibility to his friends? Is it his duty to force them into correct behavior? Looking to Scripture, we find no recorded instances of Jesus reporting or turning in any of His friends, though He was well aware of their crimes.

> *While Jesus was having dinner at Matthew's house, many tax collectors and "sinners" came and ate with Him and His disciples. When the Pharisees saw this, they asked His disciples, "Why does your Teacher eat with tax collectors and 'sinners'?" On hearing this, Jesus said, "It is not the healthy who need a doctor, but the sick. But go and learn what this means: 'I desire mercy, not sacrifice.' For I have not come to call the righteous, but sinners"* (MATTHEW 9:10-13).

Christians are to be a living example of God's power:

> *You are the salt of the earth. But if the salt loses its saltiness, how can it be made salty again? It is no longer good for anything, except to be thrown out and trampled by men* (MATTHEW 5:13).

Salt not only seasons food but creates a thirst. Christians should live in such a way as to create a thirst for the Living Water. *"In the same way, let your light shine before men, that they may see your good deeds and praise your Father in heaven"* (MATTHEW 5:16).

The Apostle Paul described the kind of example Christians should be:

> *In everything set them an example by doing what is good. In your teaching show integrity, seriousness, and soundness of speech that cannot be*

condemned, so that those who oppose you may be ashamed because they have nothing bad to say about us (TITUS 2:7-8).

KEY QUESTIONS

1. Do you think Gary would or should have acted differently if the cheating students weren't close friends?

2. Are the cheating students taking the first step down to a life of deceit and shortcuts? What about Gary Wilson? Is his moral fiber being weakened by keeping silent?

3. Are you more upset when medical students cheat than, say, students of history or English literature?

4. What does it mean to be a Christian witness? Is that an active or a passive stance? In other words, is Gary Wilson being a true Christian witness by quietly doing what is Christlike, or should he be more vocal in proclaiming Christ?

5. How do friendship and loyalty stack up against reporting your friends' wrongdoing?

6. Did Gary Wilson stand to gain anything by keeping quiet about the stolen test? If so, what?

7. What other options were open to Gary Wilson when he found out about the filched final?

THE FINAL ANALYSIS

Christian teaching has long recognized that some sins you commit by doing something you know is wrong (sins of commission). You might also sin by failing to do something you know is right (sins of omission). Gary Wil-son is called into question not so much for what he did but for what he didn't do.

We may disagree with Gary's action—or inaction. But we can also hope that he acted in the best interest of

THE CASE OF THE FILCHED FINAL

his study group friends and not merely because he was afraid to report the exam theft or unwilling to accept his friends' rejection.

Gary may be acting out of sincere Christian conscience. Perhaps having to make a decision in this tough situation will teach him to be *more* sensitive in the continuing struggle between right and wrong. We want to have faith in Gary's ability to judge *future* situations on their own merits and arrive at the best decision possible each time.

Still, there is the fact that by doing nothing, Gary is allowing cheating to occur when he could do something to stop it. Doctors are expected to hold to the highest ethical standards in practicing their profession. Gary's decision not to report the filched final could be seen by his classmates as a compromise of those ethical standards. His friends might interpret Gary's silence as approval of their cheating.

BRINGING IT HOME: THE APPLICATION

The problem of cheating isn't very far removed from our everyday lives. Every student has had to deal with the temptation in one way or another. Some teachers are so careless that it's easy to figure out foolproof ways to sneak in answers during tests or copy someone else's paper. Other times, classes are so difficult that the pressure to cheat is nearly unbearable. For every student who studies hard, there's another student who is content to copy. How many students have read "Cliff's Notes" instead of *Tale of Two Cities* or bluffed their way through a book report having read only the book's jacket?

Later, we find that it is very tempting to fudge a little bit on an income tax return, knowing full well that getting caught is highly unlikely. Cheating on resumes has become such a problem among job-seekers that employers are now hiring special investigators to verify information such as educational background and previous salary.

In the world of business, salesmen and management personnel routinely cheat on their expense reports, turning in receipts for meals and lodging that are inflated or totally false. And we even read about news reporters who invent sources of information in order to have more interesting stories.

So, cheating is common practice in today's world. But what should be the response of those who choose not to take part? Do you have a clear responsibility when faced with a choice like Gary Wilson's?

There is definitely a right way to act when confronted with a "no-win" situation such as Gary's. You can discover what God wants you to do, in your particular situation, by seeking to learn God's will through prayer, Bible study, the advice of Christian friends, personal conscience, values, and the law of love.

These decisions are not easy. In Gary Wilson's dilemma, to tell is to bring disaster to his friends. By remaining silent he deceives the faculty and other students about the fairness of the final exam. But this is the tension that Christians often live in. In the end our actions must be judged by the two greatest commandments: love God with all your heart, and love your neighbor as yourself.

THE APPEAL: REOPENING THE CASE

Now go back and reread the "Case of the Filched Final" at the beginning of this chapter. Once again, give your verdict and the reasoning behind your decision.

Do you find for the:
☐ Prosecution?
☐ Defense?

THE CASE OF THE FILCHED FINAL

Why?

Did your decision change? Did your reasoning?

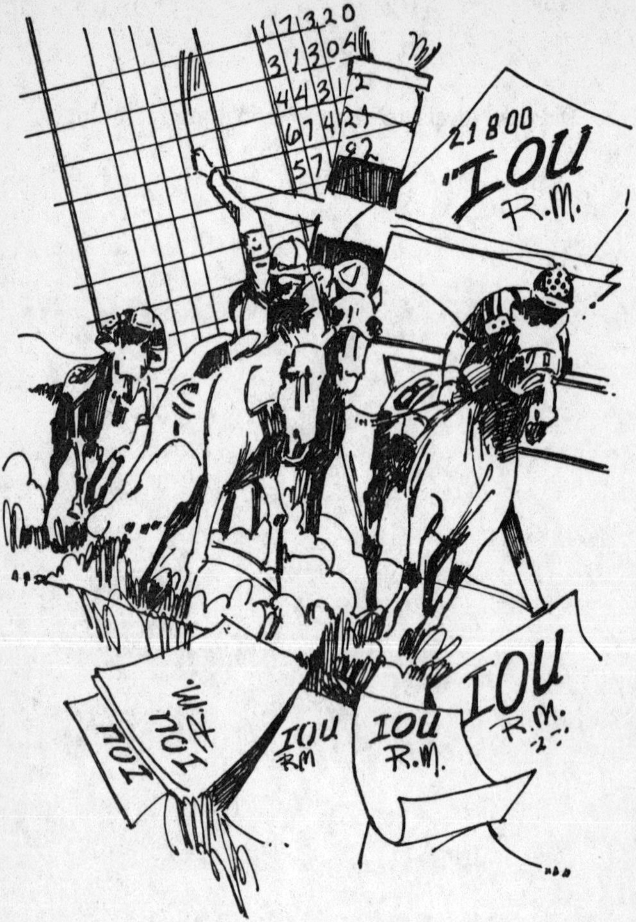
21800
IOU
R.M.
IOU
RM
IOU
R.M.
IOU
R.M.

8. THE CASE OF THE GAMBLING GUARDIAN

THE FACTS OF THE CASE

Ramsey Marsh, founder of the Christian Students' Scholarship Foundation (CSSF), was the well-respected head of an organization that for twenty-eight years had helped thousands of young people prepare for full-time Christian service. Ramsey Marsh was also a thief.

At an emergency meeting the CSSF Board of Trustees listened in shocked silence to the details of a recent audit which uncovered the loss of $30,000. They learned that the funds had been "borrowed" by Marsh, who had been in charge of CSSF bookkeeping.

When faced with the evidence, Marsh had confessed that he was a compulsive gambler. Over the years he had racked up huge gambling debts. In desperation he had taken money from the CSSF general fund to pay his debts. He meant to give the money back, but only embezzled more as his debts grew. Now, the board was informed that Ramsey had no funds to repay the $30,000 and no plans to recover the organization's money.

The Board of Trustees was split on how the situation should be handled. Several members thought that Ramsey should be fired and taken to court. After all, the organization had a responsibility to its donors, students, and the government to report the crime that had been committed.

There was a great deal of debate, lasting for hours. Finally, Richard Murdock spoke. Murdock had been one of the students helped by the CSSF and was now the pastor of a large church in Portland, Oregon.

"We're all upset by this and with good reason. But I want to tell you something about Ramsey Marsh. He's been like a father to me over the years. He took a chance on me, just like he takes a chance on the horses. Only in my case, it was the best thing that ever happened to me. The man is sick; He has a disease. If he could stop gambling, he would. We should support him in that effort, just as he's supported so many others who needed help through the years."

Heads nodded in agreement as Murdock continued. "I propose that we encourage Ramsey to get the help he needs to stop gambling. Let's each pray for him daily. And let's keep better tabs on what is happening in this office on a day-to-day basis so that he isn't tempted beyond his endurance again. I propose that we say nothing of what has happened to anyone—including Ramsey's family, the other employees, the supporters of this fine organization, and the legal authorities. I say we should accept his sincere apology, forgive *and* forget, and get on with the business we have to do."

The Board voted in favor of Richard Murdock's proposal, and no more was said of the matter.

CHARGES: The Board of Trustees stands accused of failure to prosecute a known criminal, showing disregard and disrespect for the law of the land.

THE CASE OF THE GAMBLING GUARDIAN

THE ARGUMENTS

PROSECUTION: Interestingly, Ramsey Marsh is not on trial in the Court of Ethical Appeals. We know that he is guilty of embezzlement. Indeed, it is the members of the Board of Trustees who stand accused, and they are, regrettably, as guilty as Marsh. The Board is guilty of failing to report a crime and guilty of a conspiracy of silence to cover up that crime which affects everyone associated with the Christian Students' Scholarship Foundation.

First, the Board has a legal obligation to report a crime. Marsh's embezzlement is grand larceny! Having knowledge of such a felony, they must speak up. They are hiding a criminal—a matter outside of the Board's rights and powers. The instruction to "render unto Caesar that which is Caesar's" certainly applies here!

Second, the Board of Trustees must protect the concerns of those who have given their hard-earned money to the CSSF because they wished to help needy students prepare for ministry. When donors, employees, and other interested people are kept in the dark about misuse of funds by a gambling guardian, they are being deceived. That Marsh should be allowed to remain executive director of the foundation he cheated is absurd!

It is vital that charitable organizations keep all their affairs open and above board. When dishonesty is uncovered, it must be exposed. The consequences must be accepted as the price of carelessness on the part of the Board of Trustees. Of course, it may hurt and cause embarrassment, but honesty is still the best policy.

Ramsey Marsh stole from God when he embezzled the $30,000. That money was meant to further Christian work. What right do a few insiders have to privately decide to leave such an abominable act unreported?

Indeed, Ramsey Marsh is a rather pathetic figure. He has asked for forgiveness, and it should certainly be given to him. But he is also a self-confessed criminal.

Who is served by hiding this fact? Perhaps when Marsh's crime is exposed to the light of day, he will change his ways. The Board of Trustees members failed in their legal and moral duty when they decided to participate in the cover-up of the gambling guardian.

DEFENSE: The prosecution would do well to read the Bible more carefully. The Board of Trustees acted in keeping with Scripture. They followed the teaching which says Christians are not to bring their disputes into secular courts of law. Instead, Christians are to resolve differences in a spirit of love and forgiveness.

True forgiveness is not consistent with seeking revenge through criminal prosecution. To expose Marsh's embezzlement would be to say, in effect, "You are no longer our concern. We are turning you over to the law because we will not accept any responsibility for your behavior. We reject you because of what you have done." Such words would show a response based on anger, not love. It is better to be on the receiving end of a swindle and accept the loss than to retaliate against a fellow Christian.

When private problems become public knowledge, shame is brought on the Christian community. Critics, doubters, and atheists are simply given more ammunition to fire against believers. Every public scandal involving Christian institutions hurts our credibility and weakens our witness.

To expose Marsh's sin would needlessly ruin the fine work of the Christian Students' Scholarship Foundation. To keep the problem "in the family" is not a cover-up or conspiracy of silence. Rather, it is the practice of discretion and the exercise of love, acceptance, and forgiveness.

We can be certain that God has forgiven Ramsey Marsh of his sin. How can the Board of Trustees do less? Christians ought to treat fallen brothers with the same

THE CASE OF THE GAMBLING GUARDIAN

measure of grace and forgiveness that they have received. The Board of Trustees acted correctly in the "Case of the Gambling Guardian."

YOU BE THE JUDGE

What is your verdict? Do you find for the:
- [ ] Prosecution?
- [ ] Defense?

Why? Explain your reasoning.

CASE BACKGROUND

Two issues are present in the "Case of the Gambling Guardian." We must consider the bounds of forgiveness as well as the use of civil law within the community of faith. Let's first look at forgiveness.

The call to forgive is ever present in Scripture:

> *If your brother sins, rebuke him, and if he repents, forgive him. If he sins against you seven times in a day, and seven times comes back to you and says, "I repent," forgive him* (LUKE 17:3-4).

There is little argument on this point. Both the prosecution and the defense are in favor of forgiving Ramsey Marsh. However, they disagree when it comes to what should be done *after* the forgiveness.

The prosecution believes that a "tough love" approach is called for. We see an example of this stern discipline in Acts 5:1-11. The passage tells of Ananias and Sapphira, who sold property and gave only a portion of the proceeds to the apostles, claiming it was the full amount. For this serious sin against the early church they were both instantly struck down dead.

The Apostle Paul was very severe with those inside the church who were guilty of the kinds of sin that brought shame to the body of Christ.

But now I am writing you that you must not associate with anyone who calls himself a brother but is sexually immoral or greedy, an idolater or a slanderer, a drunkard or a swindler. With such a man do not even eat (1 CORINTHIANS 5:11).

As to the question of how Christians should behave regarding matters that involve the legal system, we read this:

Is it possible that there is nobody among you wise enough to judge a dispute between believers? But instead, one brother goes to law against another— and this in front of unbelievers! The very fact that you have lawsuits among you means you have been completely defeated already. Why not rather be wronged? Why not rather be cheated? Instead, you yourselves cheat and do wrong, and you do this to your brothers
(1 CORINTHIANS 6:7-8).

On the basis of this Scripture, the defense claims that it is better for the Christian Students' Scholarship Foundation to be wronged and cheated by Ramsey Marsh than for them to shame themselves by going to court against a brother.

The prosecution referred to Christ's words, *"Give to Caesar what is Caesar's, and to God what is God's"* (MATTHEW 22:21). That assumes that grand larceny definitely comes under the heading of "what is Caesar's" since civil laws have authority over the actions of Christians (ROMANS 13:1-5; 1 PETER 2:13-14). The

THE CASE OF THE GAMBLING GUARDIAN

prosecution argues that the Board of Trustees must show their own support of law enforcement by obeying laws that relate to them. In this case they must report the serious crime of embezzlement.

KEY QUESTIONS

There are, obviously, legal questions that arise from the "Case of the Gambling Guardian." Some of these are beyond the scope of our discussion. However, we should repeat that a person with knowledge of a crime is required to report it.

The legal system of the United States is set up in such a way that what might appear to be a private offense, such as stealing money from a foundation, is also a public concern since many people's donations are involved. A government representative will bring charges against criminals regardless of whether the injured party wishes to do so or not.

Let's consider these related ethical questions:

1. Do you accept the sincerity of Ramsey Marsh's statement that he is a "sick man" and that his gambling is a disease?

2. How might a person be forgiven and still be made to pay for his sin?

3. In this situation, what is the difference between initiating a cover-up and exercising discretion?

4. Should Ramsey Marsh have turned himself in to the legal authorities? Was he right to let the Board of Trustees make that decision for him?

5. If you had been giving money to the Christian Students' Scholarship Foundation for many years, would you want to prosecute Ramsey Marsh?

6. Is there a difference between swindling a religious charitable organization and cheating the government or a big business?

7. Can you think of other options open to the Board of Trustees besides the ones presented?

THE FINAL ANALYSIS

This case involves questions of authority and loyalty. We've explored those already in the "Case of the Family Feud" and the "Case of the Filched Final." In this case we must weigh one issue against the other.

Should the trustees keep quiet about their knowledge of embezzlement out of loyalty? Or should they bow to authority and blow the whistle on Marsh? The problem is that if they say nothing, *they* break the law. They also keep all their donors in the dark as to what is going on at the Foundation. However, if the trustees turn Marsh over to the police, they open themselves and their entire organization to ridicule and criticism.

The trustees want to forgive Marsh. They seem to believe that they can't truly forgive him if they also prosecute him. After all, Christ doesn't make us pay for our sins once we ask for and accept His forgiveness.

If we are to behave in a Christlike way, what right do we have to come down so hard on Ramsey Marsh? Isn't he just a sick man who would like to stop gambling but cannot? If the courts got hold of him, they probably would not be so compassionate. Marsh would be convicted on the basis of the evidence against him. As a result his family and the CSSF would be humiliated, and the cause of Christ would suffer.

How the Board of Trustees handles this problem will largely determine whether or not it becomes a "scandal." It will be a scandal if vital information is withheld from concerned parties. It is wrong if the Board's silence is the result of an attempt to protect one person's reputation without regard for others. And if justice and forgiveness are sacrificed to either revenge or timidity,

THE CASE OF THE GAMBLING GUARDIAN

the Board has failed to do its moral duty.

BRINGING IT HOME: THE APPLICATION

Most of us know about laws that are broken. We're aware of kids who cheat in school, use drugs, or shoplift. Most of us also look the other way, believing we aren't accountable for the actions of others.

We want the law to stay out of our lives. And no matter how many times we hear that Dan the Policeman is our friend, we still get nervous when we see a patrol car in the rearview mirror. We want to handle our own problems in our own ways. We don't want a police officer to quiet down a loud party or remind us that our car's muffler has fallen off. We think of law enforcement agencies as watchdogs over other people—not us.

But such a posture has its price. If we want to handle the wrongs against us by forgiving, then we must make sure that our forgiveness includes a concern for *everyone* involved. We must not offer some sort of cheap pardon in place of real Christian love and caring.

THE APPEAL: REOPENING THE CASE

Now go back and reread the "Case of the Gambling Guardian" at the beginning of this chapter. Again, give your verdict and the reason for your decision.

Do you find for the:
☐ Prosecution?
☐ Defense?
Why?

Did your decision change? Did your reasoning?

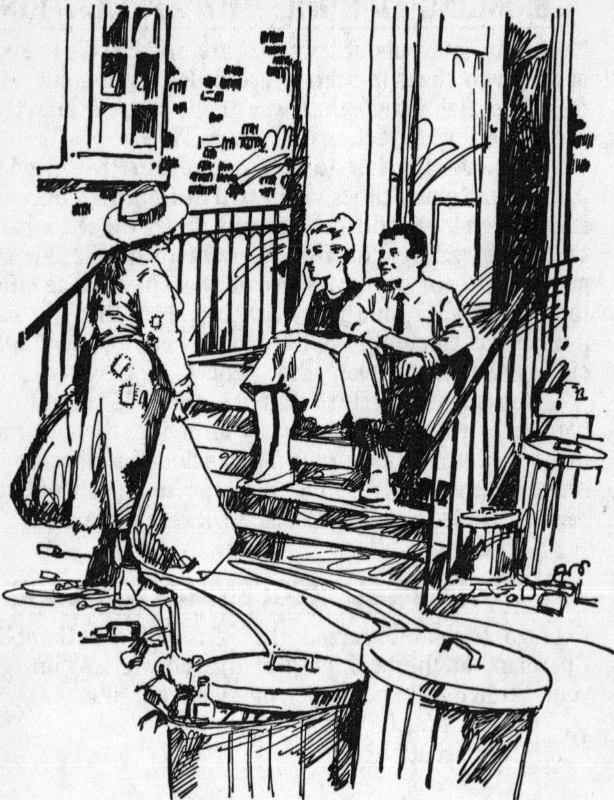

9. THE CASE OF THE TRUSTING TRIMBLES

THE FACTS OF THE CASE

The East Side of the city was once a bustling middle-class neighborhood. Now its burned-out buildings are covered with street-gang graffiti. Between vacant lots stand condemned apartment buildings. These shelter homeless street people seeking places to sleep: prostitutes, alcoholics, drug addicts, and runaways.

No one *wants* to live on the East Side. They just end up there and then wonder how to get out.

Perhaps the only two exceptions are Bob and Janet Trimble. They first moved downtown so Bob could attend graduate school in the city. The newlyweds thrived on the city's energy and excitement. They spent all their free time and extra money sampling the delicacies of ethnic restaurants and exploring out-of-the-way neighborhoods. What began as a search for adventure and new experiences finally changed their lives. Their hearts were deeply touched by the poverty and despair they witnessed in the inner city.

When Bob finished his Master's Degree in Educational Psychology, the couple moved from campus housing to the East Side. They found an inexpensive apartment in a run-down building. Bob got a job as a guidance counselor at a nearby school.

Bob's pay was enough to cover expenses, so Janet's earnings as a physical therapist at County Hospital went to help the poor and needy in their neighborhood. The Trimbles also gave 10 percent of Bob's salary to their church, living on about one third of their combined earnings.

The Trimble's small, crowded apartment seemed to have a revolving door open to anyone in need. They shared food with friends who "happened" to drop by at mealtime. They helped job-seekers fill out applications and write resumés. Children who were having trouble in school were counseled and tutored. Neighbors—drawn by the Trimbles' generosity—studied the Bible around Bob and Janet's dining room table.

They had no life insurance and decided not to pay the cost of health insurance. Instead they gave that money to overseas relief work. Their apartment was filled with broken, cast-off furniture, and they bought their clothes at secondhand thrift stores. The Trimbles were determined to live by faith and in the same lifestyle as their poorer neighbors.

Trouble came when Janet discovered she was pregnant. She told her parents the baby would be born at home and delivered by a nurse-midwife. Janet's mother—already upset about the Trimbles' lifestyle—could no longer hide her anger.

"Now it's time to quit playing Mother Theresa and behave responsibly," said Mrs. Miller. "Think of your baby! You are putting that innocent child in danger by not giving birth in a hospital. What if you need medical help? And later on you won't be able to send your kids out on the street! You owe it to your family to get out of

THE CASE OF THE TRUSTING TRIMBLES

that dangerous neighborhood and live like normal people. Don't make your children suffer for your convictions. They deserve better than this!"

These pleas fell on deaf ears. The Trimbles' first child was born in their apartment as was their second baby. Janet continued her work as a physical therapist, placing the children in the day care center for hospital employees.

By the time both of their children were of school age, Bob and Janet had lived on the East Side for ten years. During that time their home had been burglarized three times—once while they were in it. Janet had been robbed at gunpoint while shopping for groceries. The children had been harassed and beaten up by gang members. The family had run up large medical bills—still unpaid—connected with their youngest child's appendectomy. And the neighborhood continued to change for the worse.

None of this, however, weakened the Trimbles' resolve to stay in their crowded apartment. They continued to give away two thirds of their earnings and planned to live on the East Side for the rest of their lives.

CHARGES: Bob and Janet Trimble are accused of neglecting their duty to their children.

THE ARGUMENTS

PROSECUTION: The Trimbles are guilty of a sinful selfishness. This is evident in their extremist lifestyle that denies their responsibilities to their family.

If the Trimbles had no children, we might excuse their unusual behavior. But they chose to have a family of their own. This decision opens their actions to close inspection.

Old and New Testament Scriptures emphasize a person's duty to his family. The Apostle Paul went so far as to tell Timothy that the man who does not provide for his family is worse than an infidel! When a person ignores and neglects those closest to him, he misses the whole point of true love.

Charity begins at home. The Trimbles' Christian faith is less believable when they are unwilling to provide even the basics for their children's safety and well-being.

Their impractical idealism has already backfired. They have large, unpaid medical bills for an appendectomy. What if a child develops a serious illness in the future—cancer, or some other long-term condition? And what if one or both parents dies or is disabled? What then of the "faith" that failed to provide for their family with adequate health and life insurance?

When the Trimbles wind up on the welfare roles, or become a burden to their parents, who will pay the price of their do-goodism then? They will become takers instead of givers. There will be no excuse for the poor use they have made of their talents or for the neglect of their children.

DEFENSE: The Trimbles are, of course, innocent of all charges. They know that everything they have—everything they are—belongs to God and can be used to further the work of His kingdom. But only if they become vessels of His love. They reject two ideas that most of us hold dear: that we are entitled to *any* of this world's pleasures, and that anything other than complete submission to God's will is required of us. They have chosen to invest heavily in eternal goods.

Let us first point out that the Trimble children are not being neglected or abused. They have Christian parents who love and care for them, providing for their basic physical needs. Just compare these children with the needy around the world. It is plain to see that they

THE CASE OF THE TRUSTING TRIMBLES

have more than most, even if they don't live in the suburbs, attend a private Christian school, and sleep in separate bedrooms filled with expensive toys. No, let us agree that the Trimble children have an excess of what really counts—love—and that their physical needs are well met.

Most of us are busy ignoring the troubles of this world. Perhaps one Christian in a thousand takes the words of Christ seriously. We don't come across these dedicated Christians very often. We do, in fact, avoid them because they make us uncomfortable. They don't criticize us for not living as they do, but their actions convict us. We should be thankful for people like the Trimbles who quietly continue doing the Lord's will, being Christ in the world.

Remember that it was not Christ who said, "Charity begins at home." Christ said, *"Sell all that you have and follow Me."* Christ said, *"You cannot serve two masters."* Christ said, *"Deny yourself and take up My cross."*

The real crime is that more of us aren't "self-indulgent extremists" like Bob and Janet Trimble.

YOU BE THE JUDGE

What is your verdict? Do you find for the:
- [ ] Prosecution?
- [ ] Defense?

Why? Explain your reasoning.

CASE BACKGROUND

There are so many strong Scriptures that deal with giving our material possessions and our help to those in need, that we couldn't hope to mention them all. But we can begin our discussion by relating the well-known story of the rich young ruler:

> *Now a man came up to Jesus and asked, "Teacher, what good thing must I do to get eternal life?"*
>
> *"Why do you ask Me about what is good?" Jesus replied. "There is only One who is good. If you want to enter life, obey the commandments."*
>
> *"Which ones?" the man inquired.*
>
> *Jesus replied, " 'Do not murder, do not commit adultery, do not steal, do not give false testimony, honor your father and mother,' and 'love your neighbor as yourself.' "*
>
> *"All these I have kept," the young man said. "What do I still lack?"*
>
> *Jesus answered, "If you want to be perfect, go, sell your possessions and give to the poor, and you will have treasure in heaven. Then come, follow Me."*
>
> *When the young man heard this, he went away sad, because he had great wealth* (MATTHEW 19:16-22).

It has been said that we are not to assume from this incident that *all* Christians are to sell all they have. But we must rid ourselves of whatever it is—money, ambition, pride, etc.—that keeps us from fully serving God. In this instance Christ knew that the young man was devoted to his material goods, and that is why He mentioned giving it all away. Christ was right in His evaluation, since the young man went away sad.

THE CASE OF THE TRUSTING TRIMBLES

Let's be truly honest. Wouldn't each of us go away sad if we were told to sell *all* our possessions and give *eveything* to the poor in order to be perfect in God's sight? If the answer is yes, then we can't get off the hook simply by making Jesus' words about material possessions stand for anything that has too much importance in our lives. Even though that may be true, it is also true that our possessions have a special power over most of us. It is almost always our possessions that we value more highly than we should.

Several Scriptures hint about who will be rewarded and who will be punished when we are finally judged on how we lived our lives on earth. The most dramatic and clear picture of this can be found in the Gospel of Matthew.

Jesus is telling His disciples that He will one day judge all the people. He'll divide them into two groups—the righteous on His right and the others on His left. Those on the right will be blessed and inherit the kingdom, because they gave to strangers who were in need. But for the others it's a different story:

> Then He will say to those on His left, "Depart from Me, you who are cursed, into the eternal fire prepared for the devil and his angels. For I was hungry and you gave Me nothing to eat, I was thirsty and you gave Me nothing to drink, I was a stranger and you did not invite Me in, I needed clothes and you did not clothe me, I was sick and in prison and you did not look after Me."

> They also will answer, "Lord, when did we see You hungry or thirsty or a stranger or needing clothes or sick or in prison, and did not help You?"
> He will reply, "I tell you the truth, whatever you did not do for one of the least of these, you did not

do for Me."

Then they will go away to eternal punishment, but the righteous to eternal life (MATTHEW 25:41-46).

In this passage we see the importance placed on helping others.

How is this duty affected by family responsibilities? Certainly there are times when a parent will be prevented from helping someone else because his or her own child is in need. The Apostle Paul said it is good for a man *not* to marry. He recognized that the single person will not have family needs that stand in the way of following Christ.

The Roman Catholic church agrees. While acknowledging the importance of marriage and children, the Catholic church also requires priests and nuns to remain celibate and unmarried. In this way they can be fully devoted and loyal to Christ and His work.

But most people today marry and have children. This too is ordained by God and has His blessing. Does this mean the majority is giving up its right and responsibility to meet the world's overwhelming needs in order to care for close-to-home family needs?

The prosecution referred to Paul's admonition to Timothy:

If anyone does not provide for his relatives, and especially for his immediate family, he has denied the faith and is worse than an unbeliever
(1 TIMOTHY 5:8).

We can see that whatever a person says about Christ is received by nonbelievers in light of what they can see in that Christian's own life. When a person says one thing and then does another, the hypocrisy is clear

THE CASE OF THE TRUSTING TRIMBLES

to anyone watching. What that person says doesn't count for much after that. A Christian who is busy providing for the needs of others while ignoring the needs of his own family will reap all sorts of judgment—from God and from his neighbors.

But how much is enough when it comes to providing for a family? The prosecution seems to say that the Trimbles, two college graduates in professional positions, should do more for their kids. The defense wants to compare the Trimble children with the world population, showing that they already have more material goods than most people, and more love too.

The prosecution sees the lifestyle of Bob and Janet Trimble as extreme, and accuses them of irresponsibly depriving their children of basic needs. The defense, on the other hand, has a different standard. According to that standard the children have all they need. The defense says the Trimbles are doing a good job of balancing family responsibilities with the call to be Christ in the world.

KEY QUESTIONS

1. Do you agree that having children has an impact on the Trimbles' lifestyle? In what way?

2. What do you think is a basic standard of living that Christian parents should provide for their children?

3. It appears that the Trimble children are in some physical danger because of the neighborhood that they live in. Children who ride in automobiles—especially those who are not in car seats or seat belts—are also in physical danger. How do you compare those two risks? Would good parents really raise their children in a neighborhood that has gangs if they didn't have to? Would good parents really drive their children around in cars, especially when the trip was unnecessary or the

children were not restrained?

4. Do you think that your parents have made you "suffer" for their convictions in any way? How? Do you hold it against them?

5. When you hear of a Christian who has no health or life insurance, what is your first reaction? Are they stupid? Irresponsible? Misguided? Naive? Or do they have a strong faith in God?

6. Would it be ethical for a Christian who could earn a good living to live on government support because he chose not to earn as much as possible?

7. What is it about the Trimbles that you admire most? What do you disapprove of?

THE FINAL ANALYSIS

Several years ago we led a Sunday School class of young married couples. One of the members, who worked for a magazine, had recently interviewed a family very much like the Trimbles. He was personally challenged by their commitment to other people, even at the expense of their personal lives. As he told the class about this family, we noted the reactions of the other class members.

One young man, a lawyer, was appalled that this couple had made no provision for the children in the event of their deaths. He had seen parents die and leave their kids to be taken care of by poor family members or, worse yet, become wards of the state. He had also seen people lose everything they had because they didn't have enough health insurance to pay huge medical bills. He felt the couple was crazy not to pay the small cost of insurance, especially since they had the money to do so.

Another class member was a doctor. She strongly disapproved of the couple choosing a home birth instead of going to a well-equipped hospital. She compared the couple to abusive parents who beat their children. She cited the medical problems that can arise during childbirth. These problems are easily handled in a hospital but can be fatal when the delivery takes place at home.

A kindergarten teacher in the class was disgusted by the fact that these parents lived in such a bad neighborhood that they had to walk their children to school every day just to keep them from getting beat up or robbed on the way. As one who loved children, she thought that their physical safety was extremely important, and that a parent who *could* do better for her child *should* do better.

The various class members all had good reasons for feeling as they did. However, the man who had spent a week with the family was deeply moved by their faith in God's promise to meet their needs. He was impressed by their commitment to their neighborhood and their willingness to do without in order to help others.

How much is enough? What is required of a Christian? Are we expected to give a 10 percent tithe of our income back to God, or should we give more? If every Christian was poor, wouldn't that limit who could be reached by the Gospel?

We look to Scripture and find examples such as Joseph of Arimathea who provided the tomb for Christ's burial. He was wealthy, yet he served God. And when Mary anointed Christ's feet with expensive perfumes, Christ said that the poor will be with us always, and that Mary had done the right thing (JOHN 12:1-8). What do these biblical acts of giving teach us today?

BRINGING IT HOME: THE APPLICATION

Perhaps you get an allowance or have a part-time job that provides you with money you can spend pretty much as you choose. Though it might not seem like much, the way you manage it says a lot about who you are, what you value, and how you respond to the needs of others.

A certain amount of your money goes for essentials. You may buy your lunches with the allowance your parents give you or buy your own clothes with the money you earn at your job. Even though these things are necessities, you have many choices in how you spend. You can buy "plain-label" jeans instead of designer jeans or take lunches from home instead of using the school cafeteria.

Some of your money will be for extras: record albums, dates, entertainment, transportation. When you go out with other kids, do you ever pay the bill for everybody? Would you like to be able to? Look around you and you'll see some people who spend nearly everything they have on their friends and others who are always bumming, hoping not to spend anything. Sometimes this has to do with who has the money and who doesn't, but not always.

Have you ever tried to figure out what you'd do if you had a million dollars? Would you buy a car? Take a trip? Invest for the future? It wouldn't be surprising if you said that you would give away much of it—to your church, family, friends, or some worthy cause.

But the fact is, you would do with a million dollars almost exactly what you do with ten dollars. If you get ten dollars as a gift and spend it on a record album and Cokes, you would probably spend a million dollars on something for yourself with nothing left over for anything else.

But maybe when you find yourself downtown at Christmas and come upon a Salvation Army bell-ringer, you put that ten-dollar gift in the red bucket. Then it is likely that a million dollars under your control would also find its way to other people in need.

Think more carefully about the million dollars. How

THE CASE OF THE TRUSTING TRIMBLES

would you like to spend all that money? You can start by doing it with the next ten-dollar bill you get.

THE APPEAL: REOPENING THE CASE

Now go back and reread the "Case of the Trusting Trimbles" at the beginning of this chapter. Once again, give your verdict and the reasoning behind your decision.

Do you find for the:
- ☐ Prosecution?
- ☐ Defense?

Why?

Did your decision change? Did your reasoning?

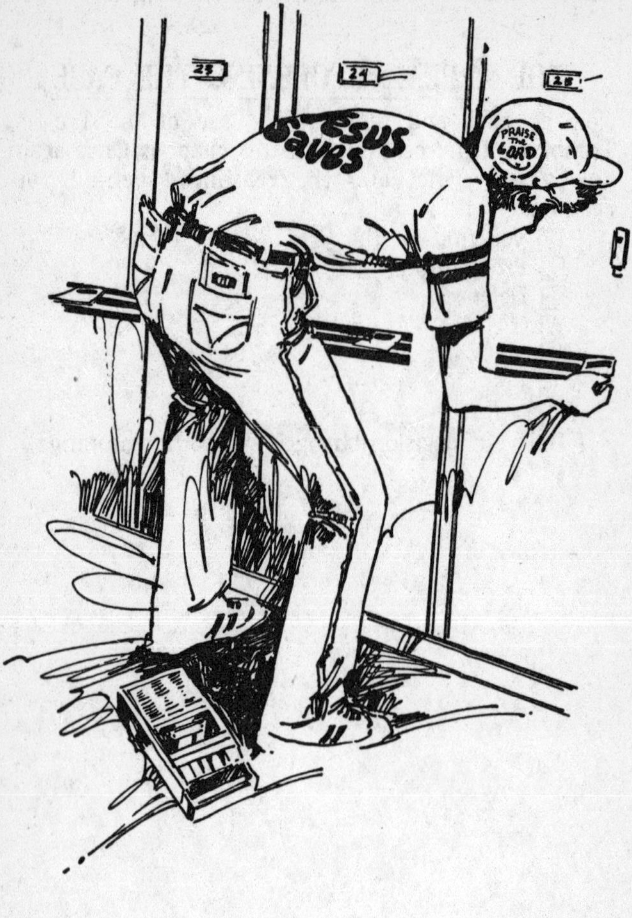

23
24
25
ESUS
Saves
PRAISE THE LORD

10. THE CASE OF THE PERSECUTED PRESSMAN

THE FACTS OF THE CASE

Dave Hammond was disappointed. After years of training he had landed a job as an apprentice binder and stitcher for the huge printing and paper company, Pennington Press. It was a great start to what he hoped was a lifetime career. But now Dave realized his dream was not turning out the way he wanted.

Even though Dave liked his work and his employer, the work environment was getting to him. He found the talk between other employees ranged from unpleasant to crude to obnoxious. The two favorite topics were who had drunk the most over the weekend and what girls in the factory were a "fun" date. Large radios blared heavy rock music the entire day. It wasn't long before all this began to wear on Dave, and he came up with a plan to fight back.

It started with T-shirts. After all, his co-workers wore T-shirts that advertised the best-loved beer or favorite rock group. So, Dave started wearing T-shirts that had a Christian message. For extra effect he added a few buttons which said "Praise the Lord" and "Smile, God Loves You."

Dave brought his own portable tape player from home with a good supply of Christian music tapes. While he worked, he liked to sing along. During breaks he found a corner of the employee lounge where he could read his Bible or some devotional book.

Before long, Dave met several other Christians in the factory. Together they asked the plant manager if they could use the employee lounge for prayer before their shift started. Permission was granted. So, three mornings a week they came to work a half hour early, shared their mutual concerns, and prayed for each other.

Dave also resolved to talk about his faith with fellow workers. He was not shy about confronting other employees with the claims of Christ and their own needs for salvation. Most of his co-workers disliked such discussions. A few became outspoken in their resentment of Dave and his use of the factory as a mission field.

Their resentment fueled the fire in the Christians, who began to meet *every* day for prayer. The Christians used the employee lounge where workers dropped off their personal belongings each day. There they would pray loudly for the salvation of certain individuals—usually when that person was in hearing range. The workers responded to this by slamming their locker doors, yelling across the room, and generally disrupting the prayer meeting.

The tension caused by bad feelings brought the issue to a head. At the monthly worker/management meeting each side presented its case.

Harvey Simon was a long-time employee who spoke for the resisters. "I resent the fact that I now dread coming to work every day knowing that I'm going to have to listen to corny hymns and fight off some guy who's trying to hound me into changing my beliefs. I

THE CASE OF THE PERSECUTED PRESSMAN

am a Jew. I don't go around saying that everyone else should be a Jew. But I'm sure not going to give up the faith that has been in my family for thousands of years. This is a free country. I should be free from religious harassment at work.

"A few years ago we decided that nonsmokers in this plant shouldn't have to breathe cigarette smoke. For the good of everyone smokers had to confine their habit to certain areas. I propose that we do the same thing with these Christians. If they want to sing hymns, and pass out tracts, and have Bible studies—fine. But they can do it on their own time. I find their behavior just as sickening as a cigarette smoker blowing smoke in my face."

Dave Hammond spoke for the Christians. "You're right; this is a free country. And if someone can show up for work with a T-shirt that says "I'm Easy," then I should be able to wear one that says "Jesus Saves." If they get to play their rock music, then why can't I sing along to my own music?

"I never force my religion on anybody. I just want to make sure that each person I meet gets to hear the Gospel message and decide whether or not to accept Christ. Fact is, if he doesn't, he's going to hell for all eternity—"

"See? That's just the sort of thing that ticks me off!" interrupted Harvey Simon.

"I do my work," Dave said, "and I do it to the best of my ability. My productivity is higher than average for this plant. I just don't see that I'm at fault in any way."

The managers and supervisors were concerned about the effect that the controversy was having on the plant's operation. They had received many complaints about the Christians. Some good employees even threatened to quit. So they made the following decisions:

- The Christians would no longer get to meet before work in the employee lounge.

- Only radios with earphones would be allowed on the job.
- There would be no religious witnessing on company property.
- Workers could continue to wear whatever message they liked on their T-shirts.

The non-Christians felt it was a fair compromise. Most of the Christians decided to abide by it too.

The next Monday morning Dave Hammond showed up for work and, for him, things went pretty much as before. He sang hymns while he worked. He introduced himself to a new worker, explaining that he was a Christian and that he wanted to talk to him about the Christian faith. During his break he stuck a tract in each employee's locker.

By 11:00 that morning he had been fired.

The next Wednesday evening he shared his story with the people in his church. It was generally agreed that Dave Hammond was the subject of religious persecution by his employer and fellow workers. They decided that he truly had suffered for the cause of Christ and was a martyr to the Christian faith.

CHARGES: Dave Hammond is accused of offending his co-workers and refusing to obey his employer, thus losing an opportunity to share Christ with others on the job.

THE ARGUMENTS

PROSECUTION: Dave Hammond is no martyr. He is an insecure and immature young man who thinks he can validate his faith by forcing people to "persecute" him for his beliefs. He asked for it and he got it.

In fact, there is no religious persecution at Pen-

THE CASE OF THE PERSECUTED PRESSMAN

nington Press, only a few obnoxious "Pharisees" and a factory full of understandably indignant workers. The workplace is not a place to force-feed co-workers religion or to confront nonbelievers with little regard for their personal freedoms.

It is, of course, an excellent place to witness—provided you do it in the right way. Real Christian faith can be demonstrated by expressing concern for co-workers who have problems and personal crises. Arriving at work each day with a smile on your face reveals the joy in your heart. Praying silently throughout the shift helps you practice the presence of God in everyday tasks. In other words, you witness best by living and working in such a way that people will beg you to tell why you are so obviously different from all those around you.

The Bible says that slaves should obey their masters. How much more should a paid employee comply with reasonable requests made by his employer? These requests are simply designed to be fair to everyone and create a pleasant working environment for all.

Dave Hammond openly disobeyed his employer and was dismissed. He cannot claim persecution or martyrdom. All he can say is that he was sacked because he refused to cooperate.

What has been gained by Dave Hammond's confrontational evangelism? Nothing, of course. No love was shown, and the Goods News of Christ was not proclaimed. Instead of befriending his co-workers, Dave offended them. Now he has been fired, and the opportunities he once had to show the love of Christ are no longer available to him.

Persecuted pressman? No, not really. The truth is, Dave is just a careless, offensive Christian who chooses to think that he is suffering nobly when really he is suffering needlessly.

DEFENSE: To persecute is to "cause to suffer

because of belief." The case of Dave Hammond is a textbook example of what happens when a committed man clashes with anti-Christian foes who try to stop the expression of his beliefs.

The "silent witness for Christ" stance proposed by the prosecution is fine as far as it goes. But it doesn't go far enough, especially when it becomes an excuse for failing to boldly proclaim Christ.

How many Christians are sitting around waiting to have others notice Christ in their lives? While they exercise their passive Christianity, the world is deprived of hearing the message of Christ. Being sensitive to others is fine but not at the price of clearly stating one's belief. All Christians are required to do as much.

Whether or not the management of Pennington Press is legally justified in making the rules it did is not a matter for this court. We wonder, though, why human philosophies such as materialism, hedonism, and humanism receive such a warm welcome in business. On the other hand, the expression of Christian beliefs is generally labeled inappropriate and out of place. Why the difference? "Freedom of religion" is quickly becoming "freedom *from* religion" in this country.

What happened to Dave Hammond is the logical outcome of living the spirit-filled life. It is a modern parallel to what happened to Peter, Paul, and other men of God who were bold in their witness. Dave Hammond has given up the approval of others, personal popularity, and his career because he dared to represent Christ in the workplace. It was a sacrifice any Christian must be ready and willing to make.

YOU BE THE JUDGE

What is your verdict? Do you find for the:
☐ Prosecution?

THE CASE OF THE PERSECUTED PRESSMAN

☐ Defense?
Why? Explain your reasoning.

CASE BACKGROUND

The word martyr comes from the Greek word *martyros*, meaning "witness." In early times being a witness nearly always led to mistreatment or persecution.

Christ tells His followers facing persecution:

> *Blessed are you when people insult you, persecute you and falsely say all kinds of evil against you because of Me. Rejoice and be glad, because great is your reward in heaven, for in the same way they persecuted the prophets who were before you* (MATTHEW 5:11-12).

The early Christians accepted intense persecution as part of everyday life. Christ—obedient until death—was followed by Stephen (stoned), Paul (beheaded), and Peter (crucified). A host of others were killed by wild animals in the Roman arena, or covered with pitch and burned as torches along the streets of Nero's Rome. Each of the apostles except Judas died a martyr's death.

In the first and second centuries after Christ's crucifixion, various methods were used to stop the spread of Christianity. Nero (A.D. 54-68) slaughtered countless Christians in Rome. Domitian (A.D. 81-96) insisted that he be addressed as "Lord and God." Trajan (A.D. 98-117) held Christians responsible for all natural disasters such as flood and famine and instructed his governor, Pliny, to execute Christians who refused to offer sacrifices to the gods. Marcus Aurelius (A.D. 161-180) had Justin the Martyr killed because he spoke out against sacrifices to the gods.

Through the ages, persecution has continued. The colonial United States was a nation formed almost entirely by people trying to escape religious persecution. Still, some groups with unpopular beliefs, including Quakers and Anabaptists, were denied civil rights and opportunities. Many were beaten and some killed for speaking openly of their particular visions of the Christian faith.

In the United States today, our government does not routinely execute outspoken Christians or deny their rights. Why is there less persecution in the U.S. than in some other countries? Answers range from the large number of Christians in our country to a special blessing that's been bestowed on the United States.

Some say the lack of religious persecution in the U.S. is a result of the remarkable spirit of tolerance and fair play which our forefathers wrote into the fabric of the Constitution. These groups side with the prosecution. They claim that in order to be martyred in *this* country one would deliberately have to make himself obnoxious, unreasonable, and uncooperative.

In a culture where there was slavery, the Bible writers instructed slaves to serve loyally.

> *Teach slaves to be subject to their masters in everything, to try to please them, not to talk back to them, and not to steal from them, but to show that they can be fully trusted, so that in every way they will make the teaching about God our Saviour attractive* (TITUS 2:9-10).

> *Slaves, submit yourselves to your masters with all respect, not only to those who are good and considerate, but also to those who are harsh* (1 PETER 2:18).

The prosecution contends that no ground was

THE CASE OF THE PERSECUTED PRESSMAN

gained by Dave Hammond's behavior. His actions did not make "the teaching about God our Saviour attractive." The prosecution argues that as a paid employee, Dave had to follow his employer's rules or accept the results.

The defense says Christians *should* be suffering persecution today just as they did 1,900 years ago. Our comfortable existence, the defense argues, is proof positive that we have failed to represent Christ to the world.

The Book of Acts is filled with examples of boldness. Peter and John were bold before the Sanhedrin. Paul spoke boldly in Jerusalem after his conversion. Paul and Barnabas spoke out for the Lord in Iconium, and Paul spoke boldly in the synagogue at Ephesus. Some form of persecution followed each incident.

KEY QUESTIONS

1. Would it be difficult or a natural thing for you to share your faith as Dave Hammond did? Have you ever had a similar experience?

2. Is there a difference between people who smoke around nonsmokers and Christians who buttonhole non-Christians? How do they compare?

3. What is the difference between "freedom of religion" and "freedom from religion"?

4. Can you think of any time when you suffered because you were a Christian? Has there been any time when you were ridiculed, ignored, deprived, or made unpopular because of your beliefs? When was the last time you took some flak for being a Christian?

5. Dave Hammond would probably get as much criticism from Christians as from non-Christians for acting as he did. Is that right?

6. With so much said in the Bible about how Christians will have to suffer because of their faith, how do you explain the fact that we do not suffer in this

country? Is it different in other countries?

7. What if Dave Hammond was a Moonie (a member of the Unification church cult) and was trying to recruit members for his church? Should he have the same on-the-job chances to witness for the Unification church as he does for Christ?

THE FINAL ANALYSIS

We have heard solid, dedicated Christians express their own disapproval of Dave Hammond-type witnessing at their place of work. Sometimes the complaints center around the fact that Christians who witness on the job are so busy doing Christ's work that they forget to do the company's work!

In the "Case of the Persecuted Pressman," however, we know that Dave's productivity is higher than average. This too sometimes makes other employees resentful. Why? Because they look bad unless they too work extra hard.

The second major complaint that Christians have against Dave Hammond-type witnessing is that it embarrasses them. Sometimes quiet Christians feel pressured to speak up, even though they don't want to. They are forced to take a stand to keep up with the outspoken believer.

Harvey Simon, the Jewish worker who spoke out in the employee meeting against Dave Hammond, stated that he had come to dread going to work because of the Christians at the factory. In this case we see that Dave Hammond's right of expression gets in the way of Harvey Simon's right to peace and quiet while he works and respect for his own beliefs. Which takes first place in this situation?

Is it more important for Dave to be an outspoken witness or for him to obey his employer's wishes? At the

THE CASE OF THE PERSECUTED PRESSMAN

bottom line we must stress that it is more important for Dave to represent Christ than to cooperate with *any* human authority.

But Dave was not faced with a black-and-white choice to either share his faith at work or not at all. He had many chances to present himself as a Christian in his life outside his work.

Remember the biblical instruction for slaves to obey their masters? Perhaps we can take that to mean it's not necessary to spend every waking hour proclaiming Christ vocally, especially when that means displeasing one's master or ignoring employer and co-worker requests.

This is not to say that a slave who obeys his earthly master is being unfaithful to God. Rather, there are times when it is important to, as Paul says, "make the teaching about God our Saviour attractive." This can be done by being a compliant, competent employee and a willing worker. Such an approach is a witness in itself.

BRINGING IT HOME: THE APPLICATION

Have you heard statements like this?

"I've just returned from Russia, where I met with Christians there. They are praying that we will also face persecution, because the persecution they've suffered has made them strong and improved their faith."

"Do you know why American Christians aren't persecuted? It's because we aren't committed! If each one of us would dedicate himself to serve God 100 percent, there would be martyrs today in this country."

Maybe you've heard this:

"God has touched this nation of ours. We have been faithful to Him and He has bestowed special blessing on us because of it. We have greater freedom, prosperity, and happiness here in the United States than anywhere on earth. It's God's hand on us for doing His will."

We know there are people in this country and around the world who are being victimized because of their faith in Jesus Christ. What about those of us who claim the same faith but are not punished for it? Does that mean that we are not as sincere, dedicated, or committed?

Seeking persecution is like trying to be humble. As soon as you say to yourself, "Hey, I'm a pretty humble guy," then you aren't anymore. Once you see humility in yourself, then you have lost it.

In the same way something's lost when you say, "Boy, I'm sure a martyr now. Look at the way they're persecuting me!"

The Apostle Paul struck the right balance. "I have learned the secret of being content in any and every situation, whether well fed or hungry, whether living in plenty or in want" (PHILIPPIANS 4:12).

The fact is, some people get nothing but the best when they do the Lord's will. There are faithful Christians who get richer and happier with each passing day. Others get heartache and trouble for their efforts. They are poor, unappreciated, and abandoned by their friends.

God deals with us individually, because He knows what is best for each of us. He works out His plan accord-ingly. What He gives to one person—good or bad—won't necessarily be given to another. That's up to Him to decide. It is up to us to try to be content in what we are doing, with little thought about whether or not this world will reward us or punish us for it.

THE APPEAL: REOPENING THE CASE

Now go back and reread the "Case of the Persecuted Pressman" at the beginning of this chapter. Once again, give your verdict and the reasoning behind your decision.

THE CASE OF THE PERSECUTED PRESSMAN 131

Do you find for the:
☐ Prosecution?
☐ Defense?
Why?

Did your decision change? Did your reasoning?

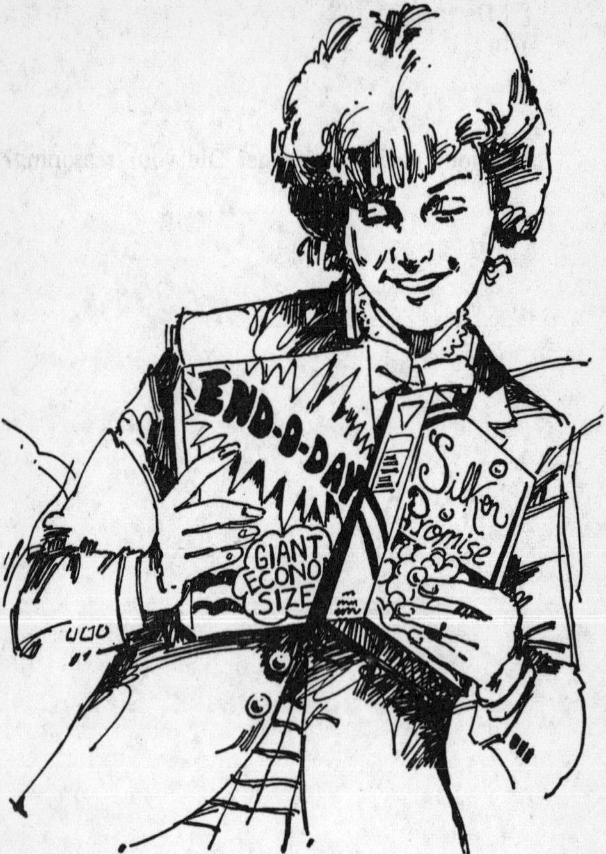
END-O-DAY
GIANT ECONO SIZE
Silken Promise

11. THE CASE OF THE DUBIOUS DETERGENT

THE FACTS OF THE CASE

"Ms. Janeway, you have done an excellent job with the Silken Promise account. Since your advertising campaign was launched, Silken Promise has indeed found its place in the market. Wilton Soap Products is *very* pleased with your work, and so are we. I am happy to say we are promoting you to Director of National Accounts for the Simmons Marketing Group."

Stephanie Janeway walked out of her boss' office about three feet off the ground. All her talent, hard work, and intuition had paid off. At the age of twenty-eight she was headed for the top.

She remembered how it was two years ago when her marketing team got the Wilton Soap account. Wilton manufactured seven laundry products sold under various labels. They also made detergent of several kinds.

The one product that badly needed help was called "End-o-Day." It was a low-priced detergent made up of the leftovers from each day's manufacturing, a mixture of all the laundry soaps Wilton produced. It was cheap, but it still didn't sell well.

When Stephanie tested End-o-Day on her own laundry she found it worked as well as Wilton's other detergents. After a few days research and thought she came up with a bold plan to give the laundry soap a whole new image. She renamed it "Silken Promise," designed a black-and-silver foil package with fancy lettering, put it in smaller boxes, and doubled the price.

At first Wilton's top management thought she had gone too far. But Stephanie Janeway convinced them that they had nothing to lose. She pointed out that the detergent cost them next to nothing to produce and that money put into advertising would be well spent.

Stephanie's plan worked, and now she had a promotion to show for it. The next day she met an old college friend for lunch and told him the details of her triumph. When she finished, he was silent.

"Nothing to say, Richard? No pat on the back?"

"Look, Steff, have you ever thought that what you did with that product might have been just a little bit dishonest?"

"Dishonest? What are you talking about? This is an advertising campaign!"

"Advertising or otherwise, you created a giant lie in order to sell an inferior product."

"It's not inferior. I used it and it was just fine. That's just the way advertising works, Richard. You look at a product, find out what's attractive about it, and make the most of it. Look, hype may get consumers to try a product. But if they don't like it, they'll quit buying it, and that will be the end of Silken Promise. It's not lying to try your best to sell your product."

"It *is* lying, Stephanie. I wish you could see that. There isn't one ethic for everyday life and another one for business."

"There sure is, and everyone knows it. There are

THE CASE OF THE DUBIOUS DETERGENT 135

business ethics and ethics for politics, sports, and a lot of other fields. Business is a game with its own set of rules. If everyone plays by the rules, no one gets hurt. I played by the rules, and I really can't understand your criticism."

The lunch ended uncomfortably for both Stephanie and Richard. Stephanie returned to the office with her mind unchanged and conducted business as usual.

CHARGES: Stephanie Janeway is accused of practicing situational ethics. She is accused of operating under the system that says certain areas—such as business and politics—are free from the basic moral laws that govern us all.

THE ARGUMENTS

PROSECUTION: Stephanie is guilty of sacrificing her standards in order to get ahead in the advertising world. She has bought into the mindset that says: "All's fair in love and war." She believes anything goes in advertising and business even when what is "fair" in business is unacceptable in other situations. When a person applies one standard of behavior to her job and another to her nonbusiness relationships and activities, then ethics have no meaning at all.

To honestly market a product is one thing, but to do so by deceit is another. And Stephanie did deceive. Those who pay extra for a product called Silken Promise expect a first-rate detergent. If you doubt this, ask a consumer how he feels about paying twice as much for Silken Promise as for End-o-Day detergent when they are exactly the same thing. See what response you get!

If advertising is a game, as Ms. Janeway suggests, it is only a game for the manufacturers, marketers, and merchandisers. It is not a game to the consumer. For it is not merely *products* that are being sold anymore, but a way of life and set of ideals.

On television we see happy young men and women sitting around a ski lodge fireplace. They raise their beer mugs and say confidently, "It doesn't get any better than this!" We watch a young couple go through a happy pregnancy and safe childbirth resulting in healthy twin babies. They turn to VISA for help with the bills. Another commercial shows us that the men and women who drink Tab Cola have the ultimate body—slim and tan.

In these ads it is not beer, credit, and soda pop that is being sold. It is happiness, health, prosperity, and Madison Avenue's idea of beauty. Americans buy the product, having been tricked into believing that they will get the image that goes along with it.

Christians, Stephanie Janeway included, should know better than to be part of such deception. She may think a separate ethic governs her business dealings, but what Stephanie does for Simmons Marketing Group soon affects the everyday lives of thousands of people. Her actions affect each person who buys Silken Promise expecting something it cannot deliver: superior performance and status. She cannot claim to be unassociated with those cheated consumers.

All this is not to say that a Christian cannot work in advertising, business, or politics, be competitive, and succeed. But a Christian must bring to his work the same ethical standards that he lives with off the job. If he fails to do so, his life is a sham.

DEFENSE: Stephanie Janeway's ethics are just fine. Situational ethics is a good concept. It recognizes that simple answers do not help us deal practically with life's complex circumstances. In order to survive, fields such as business, politics, economics, and art must be self-regulated and subject to their own standards.

THE CASE OF THE DUBIOUS DETERGENT 137

Professional standards are based on the special concerns of each field. For example, in the political arena candidates running for office sing their own praises and talk about their own virtues. They must do this so voters will see their strengths and support them because of those qualities. Then, should a candidate act the same way while golfing with his friends? No. What is standard operating procedure while addressing a political rally becomes conceited bragging when done on the golf course.

In the practice of law, a public defender will represent a guilty client, giving that person the best legal counsel possible. Does that mean that this lawyer approves of what the criminal has done? No, naturally the lawyer recognizes the difference between right and wrong. But our justice system requires that competent legal counsel be provided to anyone accused of a crime, whether that person is innocent or guilty. That's the only way the system can work.

These examples show that it is perfectly legitimate to apply specific ethics to specific situations—not for personal gain but for the good of everyone.

Now, back to Stephanie Janeway. She did what a marketing consultant is expected to do. She presented her product attractively and according to the ethical standards of her profession. Stephanie acted as though business is subject to different principles, because indeed it is. One cannot be expected to apply personal ethics to impersonal situations. There is no fault to be found in Stephanie's actions.

YOU BE THE JUDGE

What is your verdict? Do you find for the:
- ☐ Prosecution?
- ☐ Defense?

Why? Explain your reasoning.

CASE BACKGROUND

Christians, believing that love for God determines values and ethics, are nonetheless divided on the issue of situational ethics. Some say that there are only two commandments:

> *Jesus replied: " 'Love the Lord your God with all your heart and with all your soul and with all your mind.' This is the first and greatest commandment. And the second is like it: 'Love your neighbor as yourself.' All the Law and Prophets hang on these two commandments"* (MATTHEW 22:37-40).

Some believe we should apply these commandments to our lives in every situation—from personal problems to business matters.

Take the case of Daniel. He was one of the top administrators in the kingdom of Babylon. He did so well that the other administrators and officials were jealous and decided to force him out of office.

So they tricked King Darius into ruling that everyone in the kingdom had to pray to Darius for a month. Daniel, a man of God, wouldn't pray to Darius, and was thrown into the lions' den. (Remember this story?) God miraculously saved his life by shutting the lions' mouths. As a result, Darius came to believe in the true God, and Daniel once again prospered.

In this instance a man who applied his personal values to his job came out OK. Daniel refused to cooperate in petty corruption. He was persecuted for his belief in God. But eventually he triumphed over that persecution and continued successfully in his career.

The defense would say that's all very well and good, but it doesn't present the whole story. Following the two great commandments is fine, but it doesn't go far

THE CASE OF THE DUBIOUS DETERGENT

enough. We need more specific guidelines.

Certain professions develop their own ethical standards by which members of the profession are expected to conduct themselves. These standards are merely outgrowths of what is generally considered to be moral behavior.

An example of this in the Bible is the teaching about masters and slaves. These days we don't have slavery, but they had it in Bible times. The Apostle Paul said, *"There is neither Jew nor Greek, slave nor free, male nor female, for you are all one in Christ Jesus"* (GALATIANS 3:28).

Paul also instructed those who *were* masters or slaves to conduct themselves ethically *within* the framework of their station.

> *Slaves, obey your earthly masters with respect and fear, and with sincerity of heart, just as you would obey Christ. . . . Serve wholeheartedly, as if you were serving the Lord, not men, because you know that the Lord will reward everyone for whatever good he does, whether he is slave or free.*
>
> *And masters, treat your slaves in the same way. Do not threaten them, since you know that He who is both their master and yours is in heaven, and there is no favoritism with Him* (EPHESIANS 6:5, 7-9).

We might conclude that Paul, in effect, is saying something like this: "Actually, all this slavery business is bad, because it is contrary to the way God views people. He doesn't see us as slaves or masters—we're all equal in His sight. But the fact of the matter is that we *do* have slavery, and that if you are a slave or a master, the important thing is for you to do what is expected of you in whatever situation you find yourself."

The defense would say that a person who works for a marketing company is expected to do his or her best to accomplish the goals of the employer: namely, to find effective ways to sell a product. By doing so he stays in God's will, even though a good adman might occasionally do something work-related that wouldn't be appropriate in everyday life. This could include presenting only the good side of a product without talking about the bad or putting attractive packaging on the product so that its quality is overlooked by the consumer.

KEY QUESTIONS

1. Are there some jobs that a Christian would have a hard time doing because of moral or ethical conflicts? Consider the following occupations:
   - [ ] television programming executive
   - [ ] actor
   - [ ] rock musician
   - [ ] President of the United States
   - [ ] used car salesman
   - [ ] army officer
   - [ ] bill collector

Can you think of any ethical conflicts that might arise for Christians holding these jobs?

2. What advertisements do you think are dishonest? Think of specific television or print ads, or general advertising trends.

3. Is it OK to do something in business if your competitors are doing it and you need to stay competitive?

4. Do you think that Jesus, given His moral perfection, could succeed in business today?

5. Do you think most honest people succeed while the dishonest ones fail?

6. Is there another advertising campaign for

BRINGING IT HOME: THE APPLICATION

Have you ever taken an oath, repeated vows, or made a pledge?

"I pledge allegiance to the flag of the United States of America..."

"On my honor, I will do my best to do my duty..."

"I, Patricia, take thee, Robert, to be my lawfully wedded husband...."

Have you ever thought of what it means to take a pledge like that? Sometimes we just say the words and don't think about the meaning. We go through the motions because it's expected or because it's part of a ritual or ceremony.

Many pledges we take are not spoken. For instance, when you work for a company, as Stephanie Janeway works for Simmons Marketing, you promise that you will be honest in your work, won't steal from your employer, won't give company secrets to a competitor, and will do your best to help the company succeed. This pledge isn't usually in writing. You don't swear on a stack of Bibles, but the pledge is understood nonetheless.

A pledge says, "No matter what else happens, I'll do this." It creates a miniworld that is governed by its own rules. Consider a marriage vow. That is a pledge that should not be broken just because the wife finds herself attracted to another man or because the husband is tired of supporting the family. The marriage is a world of two people held together by promises kept.

Such a miniworld is also created in business. When a person commits himself to work for a company and to live by the ethics of a profession, he says, "I promise to conduct myself according to the accepted rules. Maybe it doesn't make sense to those of you looking in. But I see the logic in it because I work at this job on a day-to-day basis. Things run smoothly and operate fairly when I stick to my professional ethics."

THE CASE OF THE DUBIOUS DETERGENT

End-o-Day detergent that might sell the product and still be absolutely truthful?

THE FINAL ANALYSIS

In this book's first chapter we mentioned the "borderline case." In borderline situations, moral decisions are not always clear. We have to believe that our Christian faith and the values that go along with it will guide us when we make tough decisions on the border line.

In life's "gray areas" there are honest differences of opinion about how to best live as a Christian in a non-Christian world. Some sincerely believe that normal Christian behavior does not apply in certain areas of activity.

For example, some people think it is impossible for a Christian to serve in the armed forces. Why? Because one does not follow biblical directions to "turn the other cheek" and "repay evil for good" by taking part in a military attack. Others say that those instructions and the commandment "Thou shalt not kill" are suspended during time of war.

Do you agree with people who think a Christian could never be a rock musician? They believe that rock music defies the Christian faith, mocks Christian tradition, and encourages young people to rebel against parents and authority. Others say that is only partly true. They argue that a committed Christian can create and perform rock music without having to compromise Christian values.

Another example involves Christian politicians. Some people think that by nature politics can only exist when deals are made, convictions are compromised, and truth consistently warped. Others say that Christian politicians are vitally needed for responsible government that reflects Christian values and opinions.

THE CASE OF THE DUBIOUS DETERGENT 143

In the "Case of the Dubious Detergent," Stephanie had made a pledge to her employer to do her very best. She was only doing her duty in promoting Silken Promise soap. She did stay within the ethics of advertising. But the question is, did she stay within the bounds of Christian ethics?

Have you ever been faced with a choice between keeping a promise and carrying out your Christian commitment? Which won out? It is important to remember in these situations that we are on display no matter what we do. When our talk doesn't match our actions, people might begin to question how real our faith truly is.

THE APPEAL: REOPENING THE CASE

Now go back and reread the "Case of the Dubious Detergent" at the beginning of this chapter. Once again, give your verdict and the reasoning behind your decision.

Do you find for the:
☐ Prosecution?
☐ Defense?
Why?

Did your decision change? Did your reasoning?

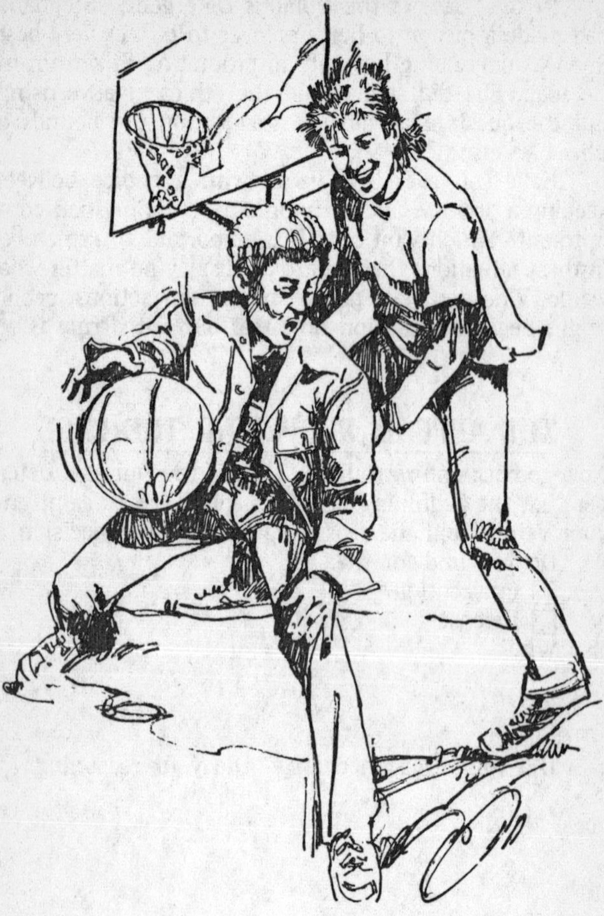

12. THE CASE OF THE LIBERATED LEADER

THE FACTS OF THE CASE

Peter Conyers seemed like the ideal person for Gordon Street Church. He was hired to expand the church's youth ministry by reaching neighborhood kids and, through them, their families. Peter's background in working with summer camping programs and his dynamic Christian faith made him an obvious choice. At first he was a big hit with church parents and young people because of his wholehearted dedication, enthusiasm, and personal charisma.

After a while, though, church opinion began to turn against Peter. It started with his Sunday-morning routine. Before church he would show up at the nearby school playground and throw baskets with the neighborhood kids. Usually he had just enough time to make it to the morning service but not enough time to change clothes or clean up. When he began to regularly come to worship in grimy sneakers and sweaty warm-ups—often bringing along similarly grubby kids—there were whispers among the congregation.

Over several months there were other changes in Peter's personal appearance. He had had his ear pierced and got a punk-style haircut (long in back, nearly shaved on top). His new look brought outspoken criticism from a number of parents. Finally, Peter was called before the Christian Education Committee to offer an explanation for his behavior.

"Peter," said the committee chairperson, "you appear a very different young man than the one we hired last year. The general feeling we're getting from church members is that the style you have adopted is one of open rebellion and total disrespect for the values of our congregation. Young people are going to get the wrong idea about what it means to be a Christian when they see you with that jade earring, your crazy haircut, and those weird clothes.

"I'll admit you are well within your *personal* right to act and dress as you choose. But you've got to realize that as a Christian with a leadership position in this church, you have a tremendous influence on our young people. They look up to you and see you as a role model. You must think first of how your behavior affects them. You must put the needs of young Christians first, even if that means sacrificing your personal freedom to dress as you choose.

"We simply cannot accept the message of rebellion that your clothes and hairstyle give out. You have bought into a worldly set of values. You've become part of a subculture that openly ridicules the teachings of Christ."

Peter, stunned by this accusation, fought to keep his voice under control.

"You hired me to develop a youth ministry for this church that would reach out to the kids in the neighborhood," he said. "That's what I'm doing. The kids don't think my appearance is unusual. If I dressed like you—in a three-piece suit and black wing tips—I wouldn't

THE CASE OF THE LIBERATED LEADER

stand a chance with them. In fact, your traditional dress is associated with middle-class materialism. I think it's a stumbling block to people in our own community who won't come to church because they think they don't have nice enough clothes to wear."

Peter took a deep breath and continued. "But that's not why I dress like this. I *like* dressing and acting the way I do. It feels right to me. The way I look and behave shows that a person can be a Christian, attend church, and still keep his individual personality. I am able to show kids that they can accept Christ without buying into middle-class ways of dressing and thinking. That's the message of Christian freedom, Folks. It's the message kids need to hear.

"Frankly, I don't like the way *you* dress and all that stands for. But you don't hear me making a big deal out of it. So you don't like pierced ears. In that case, I don't think you should get yours pierced! But don't criticize my decision to do so. It's up to me and God to work out how I will live my life."

The Christian Education Committee disagreed with that last statement. They felt that Peter Conyers had a responsibility to the church. What he called freedom, they called rebellion. For that reason, he was encouraged to find other employment and was dismissed as Youth Director of the Gordon Street Church.

CHARGES: Peter Conyers is accused of abusing his Christian freedom by putting his personal tastes and desires above the needs of the church.

THE ARGUMENTS

PROSECUTION: Peter has failed to fulfill his responsibility to the Gospel of Jesus Christ and the people of Gordon Street Church. His selfish actions have harmed the young people who view him as a role model, as well as the parents who trusted him to set a good example for their children.

Yes, we do have freedom as Christians. Yes, it is more a matter of personal taste than Christian doctrine when it comes to whether or not a young man has a pierced ear or odd haircut. But what can we say of a Christian who insists on dressing this way when it stirs up trouble in the church?

Claiming Christian freedom in such a situation twists the concept entirely. Peter Conyers is so bent on being his *own* person that he forgets he is first and always *God's* person. Of course, we are free from the Law. But we are subject to a much higher standard of behavior—love. Peter Conyers fails to show love when his life-style pushes people apart instead of bringing them together.

Obviously, Peter feels that he is strong and mature enough to dress as he does without adopting the attitudes of most "punks." That's fine for him, but what about the kids who are influenced by him? Are they strong and mature enough to resist the punk attitude? By copying their youth group leader will they get sucked into a life-style that has no point of reference with Christ? Peter must be careful not to cause his "weaker brothers" to stumble because of him.

Peter Conyers should find a way to express his individuality that will not cause such trouble within the Christian community. He can be his own person in dress and behavior without resorting to a wild appearance which stirs controversy and hard feelings. He should concentrate on being "all things to all people," so that many will be won to Christ.

DEFENSE: Peter Conyers has refused to become part of a plot to turn faith into a list of do's and don'ts

THE CASE OF THE LIBERATED LEADER

based on the likes and dislikes of one group of people.

There is a place for differing lifestyles, clothing, and personality types in the service of Christ. Yet in spite of differences we are parts of the same body. Unfortunately, in this case one part of the body, the Christian Education Committee, is insisting that another part, Peter, give up his personal ministry so he can be like them. If Peter had given in, he would have failed to let God use his special talents. He would have sold out to the misguided teaching that we should all be the same—a teaching which makes the body of Christ totally nonfunctional.

Christian freedom is at stake here. In exercising his, Peter Conyers is not causing any "weaker brother" to stumble. Rather, he is providing a real-life illustration of what it means to be made free by the Son of God.

Instead of criticizing him, the committee should be learning from him. They should be learning that the way a person looks has very little to do with who he is. They know he is an effective youth leader. Why go any further than that?

The committee hired Peter to bring neighborhood people into the life of the church. The committee should not be involved in matters unrelated to that goal. Peter is accomplishing good work in his own way, and the church ought to recognize that.

These committee members care more about Peter's outward appearance than his personal relationship with Jesus Christ. Peter recognized this trap and wisely took steps not to fall into it. By standing up to the committee, he opposed those who want to return to slavery everyone set free by the Gospel of Jesus Christ.

YOU BE THE JUDGE

What is your verdict? Do you find for the:
- ☐ Prosecution?

☐ Defense?

Why? Explain your reasoning.

CASE BACKGROUND

During Christ's ministry and later, there were people who wanted to make Christianity a sect of Judaism. They agreed that Jesus is the Messiah, but they didn't understand God's gift of grace. They were unwilling or unable to believe that Christ had caused love to replace the Jewish law. So, they demanded that non-Jewish Christians be circumcised, that certain "unclean" foods not be eaten, and that Jewish traditions be followed.

The trend is still with us today. There are those who demand certain behavior from Christians, not as an outgrowth of the Christians' faith but as a way to win God's favor.

The Apostle Paul found himself having to clarify the difference between salvation by faith and salvation by works.

> *But now that you know God—or rather are known by God—how is it that you are turning back to those weak and miserable principles? Do you wish to be enslaved by them all over again? You are observing special days and months and seasons and years! I fear for you, that somehow I have wasted my efforts on you* (GALATIANS 4:9-11).

Apparently, true freedom was a difficult concept for the early Christians to grasp.

The defense would say that it is still a difficult concept to grasp. Some people cannot seem to take hold of freedom in Christ for themselves. And they won't tolerate it in others. Like the Christian Education Committee

THE CASE OF THE LIBERATED LEADER

of Gordon Street Church, they want people like Peter Conyers to conform to certain standards.

Paul wrote that the inner person is more important than outside appearances. *"Those who want to make a good impression outwardly are trying to compel you to be circumcised.... Neither circumcision nor uncircumcision means anything; what counts is a new creation"* (GALATIANS 6:12, 15).

Peter Conyers has focused on this issue, claiming that if he is not free to dress and act as an individual, he cannot share the message of new life and freedom in Christ with neighborhood kids who need to hear it.

Both the prosecution and defense might refer to this Scripture: *"Don't let anyone look down on you because you are young, but set an example for the believers in speech, in life, in love, in faith, and in purity"* (1 TIMOTHY 4:12).

The defense could argue that Peter is being discriminated against because of his youth and youthful appearance. The prosecution would say Peter has failed to win approval in his speech, life, love, faith, and purity.

Those who are leaders in the church are instructed to behave in a manner that defies criticism:

> Now the overseer must be above reproach, the husband of but one wife, temperate, self-controlled, respectable, hospitable, able to teach, not given to much wine, not violent but gentle, not quarrelsome, not a lover of money (1 TIMOTHY 3:2-3).

> In everything set them an example by doing what is good. In your teaching show integrity, seriousness, and soundness of speech that cannot be condemned, so that those who oppose you may be ashamed because they have nothing bad to say about us (TITUS 2:7-8).

A person in leadership automatically gives up certain rights. Peter has a responsibility to the church members who hired him—not only because they are his employers, but because they too fall under his influence. The parents and children currently within the church might be misled because of Peter's behavior. If so, he has failed to show them the same love that he wants to show to young people outside the church.

As Paul has advised, we must balance freedom with love:

> *So whether you eat or drink or whatever you do, do it all for the glory of God. Do not cause anyone to stumble, whether Jews, Greeks, or the church of God—even as I try to please everybody in every way. For I am not seeking my own good, but the good of many, so that they may be saved* (1 CORINTHIANS 10:31-33).

KEY QUESTIONS

1. How does a person's appearance reflect his or her values? How do you expect the following people to look?
   - [ ] banker
   - [ ] preacher
   - [ ] rock musician
   - [ ] classical musician
   - [ ] high-school teacher
   - [ ] high-school dropout

2. Do you think that a youth minister is more responsible to adults in the church's congregation or kids he or she is working with?

3. Do you think that a person is more likely to *act* straight if he *looks* straight? Or do you think that the way a person looks is not related to how he acts?

4. Does Peter Conyers strike you as a basically ma-

THE CASE OF THE LIBERATED LEADER

ture or immature person?

5. Do you expect more from people who lead (like the President, your school principal, your minister, your class officers) than you do from other people who are not in leadership positions? If so, what should be different about these people?

6. Could Peter and the Christian Education Committee have worked this situation out some other way?

THE FINAL ANALYSIS

The tug-of-war between freedom and responsibility has been going on for a long time. There are some people who think that freedom is just too much for most people to handle, that most of us are better off with someone else making our decisions. They argue that the man on the street just can't cope with the hassle of being completely on his own.

The message of Christ truly is a message of freedom. For the Jews living around the time that Jesus was on earth, it meant that they were no longer tied to their lengthy lists of do's and don'ts. They could be saved without obeying the letter of the Law.

But the *spirit* of the Law—love—remained. Some of these first-century Jews were no doubt relieved that they didn't have to obey the Jewish Law, until they learned they now had to obey a much stricter law—that of love for God and love for one's fellowman. Some of them decided that the old Law wasn't so bad after all and went back to it trying to be saved by their works, not by their faith.

And so it is today. There are plenty of people ready and willing to tell us how to live our lives, and how to be better Christians. All we have to do is go to church five times a week, study the Bible thirty minutes every day, tithe, wear a suit, drive an American-made car, watch less television, eat natural foods, and on and on.

Everyone, it seems, has a plan for our lives. But what is God's message? His message is this:

> *"Everything is permissible"—but not everything is beneficial. "Everything is permissible"—but not everything is constructive. Nobody should seek his own good, but the good of others* (1 CORINTHIANS 10:23-24).

While we are free to do as we choose, we would be wise to think before we act, giving special consideration to how our actions will affect other people. That is not to say that our actions should be *dictated* by other people—they definitely should not. But we don't live in a vacuum. When those we love, and whom God loves, are threatened in any way by our actions, it's time to remember that our freedom brings with it the responsibility to use it wisely in serving God and others.

BRINGING IT HOME: THE APPLICATION

Do your parents like the way you look? Do they bug you about your hairstyle, clothes, or the way you talk? How about your friends? What kind of image do you project to them? Jock? Preppie? Punk? Greaser?

The way you look and act are your opportunities to express yourself. You can't stop everyone you meet on the street and tell them what a valuable player you were on the school's basketball team last season. But you can wear your letter jacket and Converse high tops, and that will tell the story. Clothes, hairstyles, and mannerisms broadcast what we are.

Outward appearances can also be a ticket to where we want to be. It's generally agreed that if you want to do well in business, you must "dress for success."

THE CASE OF THE LIBERATED LEADER

If you want to be accepted by your teachers, you need to look sharp. They'll be more impressed by corduroys and a V-neck sweater than a ripped T-shirt and cut-offs. If you want to hang out with the whiz kids, you'd better know your RAMs from your ROMs.

We each try to find out where we want to go and where God wants us to go. Once you know where you're headed, it's perfectly acceptable to use special clothes and mannerisms to get there. It is *permissible*.

Beyond that, you must determine if it is also *beneficial* and *constructive*.

THE APPEAL: REOPENING THE CASE

Now go back and reread the "Case of the Liberated Leader" at the beginning of this chapter. Once again, give your verdict and the reasoning behind your decision.

Do you find for the:
☐ Prosecution?
☐ Defense?
Why?

Did your decision change? Did your reasoning?

13. IN CONCLUSION, LADIES AND GENTLEMEN OF THE JURY

THE AWFUL TRUTH

Now that you have read this book, it's safe to go ahead and reveal the nature of its contents. If we had told you earlier, you probably wouldn't have gotten this far.

This has been an exercise in "theological ethics." It has been about how Christians operate in our society. How will a Christian act when he gets in a tough situation? Will he behave differently than a non-Christian? If so, why?

Think back to the illustration in chapter one about hiking in the Great Smokey Mountains. We pointed out that it's easy to see on a map where the border is between Tennessee and North Carolina. But it's difficult to know exactly where you are when actually stumbling around in the mountains.

Theological ethics are in the business of helping hikers find their ways. They start discussions on how to discover the right direction. They give guidance in finding out where the border line really is.

So, the awful truth is that while reading this book

IN CONCLUSION

and reacting to the cases, you've also been wading through a lot of dry, dusty philosophy on the subject of theological ethics.

DEBRIEFING

Do any of the following statements sum up what you think?

- The Bible can be used to prove almost anything. It's chock-full of contradictions and statements that no one can understand.
- There really isn't any such thing as absolutely right or absolutely wrong. Everything depends on your point of view.
- Life is so confusing that you'd be a fool to try and figure it out.
- All this "borderline" business is for the birds. What it really means is that when you come up against a tough decision, you lose no matter what you do.

Even though such reactions are normal, we hope that you won't make them a big part of the way you view life. These are defeating, useless ways to approach tough problems, because they encourage you to give up. That doesn't solve anything.

We hope you came to some of the following conclusions:

- There is a lot in Scripture that can help you deal with problems in your life. But it isn't enough just to casually read a verse or two. You really have to read the Bible with respect. You have to study hard to find out what it's saying.
- It's important to keep thinking about the two great commandments: love God and love your neighbor as yourself.
- The two great commandments are hard to fol-

low, but when all is said and done, they make the most useful guideline to go by.

● When you find yourself in a borderline situation, it's a terrific opportunity to show the world that there's something special about the way Christians handle life's problems.

If you can close this book thinking along these lines, then you have come a long way toward understanding how to deal with life's "gray areas." This book can't tell you how to solve the problems of your personal borderline situations, but it can help you learn to understand and get through them.

GUILTY AS CHARGED

Whenever we make a decision in a borderline situation, most likely we're going to end up feeling guilty.

For example, consider the "Case of the Devastated Detective." If Michael Ortiz quits the police force, he will feel guilty for abandoning his duty to his community. If he stays on the force, he will feel guilty for behaving immorally and breaking his own behavior code.

In the "Case of the Filched Final," if Gary Wilson reports his friends' cheating, he will feel guilty for his disloyalty. If he keeps quiet about their activities, he will feel guilty for his dishonesty.

Remember the "Case of the Dissenting Deacon"? If Roger Erickson leaves his church, he will feel guilty for his failure to exercise tolerance and Christian unity. Should he stay in his church, he will feel guilty for supporting poor stewardship and participating in an activity he believes is wrong.

No matter what we do, we'll feel guilty as charged. Like the characters in this book, we find ourselves in situations where even though we think we're doing the right thing, we end up feeling guilty for something else.

IN CONCLUSION

What can we do about that? Do we have to be miserable all the time, constantly hounded by the fear that we've done the wrong thing? Must we believe there is nothing we can do to justify our actions and continue feeling rotten because we have so much on our consciences?

No, we have another alternative. We can claim the forgiveness that God has promised. We can say this to God:

"I had to make a hard choice today. I didn't know what to do. I had to choose between _____ on the one hand and _____ on the other. I read my Bible. I prayed. I talked to my closest friends about it. In the end, I decided that the right thing would be to _____. I know that the full responsibility for what happened isn't on my shoulders anymore. I claim Your forgiveness for the part of the decision that may have been displeasing to You. I thank You for being with me and loving me through it all."

THE REPRIEVE

We trust that God understands the difficulty under which we are operating. Knowing that He is ready, willing, and able to forgive us should inspire a great deal of confidence as we live our day-to-day lives.

Our actions cannot always be right. It's impossible. But *we* can be right—right with God. That's the most important thing.

It's not nearly as bad to fall down as it is to fall away. We fall *down* all the time. We make mistakes, get lazy, or mess up when we could have done better. But as long as we haven't fallen *away* from God and are trying to do the right thing, we can be certain of His love for us and His willingness to forgive us.

It's a great life! We can face life's tough situations

with help from the Bible, our Christian friends, and direct assistance from God. We can approach those borderline situations with confidence, knowing that *nothing* will separate us from the love of God. We can look at them as a great opportunity to put our faith into action and show other people why it's such an exciting thing to be a Christian.